# PIERRE REVERDY

## *Poems Early to Late*

# PIERRE REVERDY

## *Poems Early to Late*

Edited and Translated by

Mary Ann Caws and Patricia Terry

BLACK
WIDOW
PRESS

Pierre Reverdy: Poems Early to Late

Black Widow Press is an imprint of Commonwealth Books, Inc., Boston, MA. Distributed to the trade by NBN (National Book Network) throughout North America, Canada, and the U.K. All Black Widow Press books are printed on acid-free paper, and glued into bindings. Black Widow Press and its logo are registered trademarks of Commonwealth Books, Inc.

Joseph S. Phillips and Susan J. Wood, Ph.D., Publishers
www.blackwidowpress.com

Text Design & Production: Kerrie Kemperman

ISBN-13: 978-0-9960079-5-5
Printed in the United States

10 9 8 7 6 5 4 3 2 1

# TABLE OF CONTENTS

Selection from *Le Cadran Quadrillé (The Gridded Dial)*, 1915
tr. Mary Ann Caws

Selection from *Quelques poèmes (Some Poems)*, 1916
tr. Mary Ann Caws

Selection from *La Lucarne ovale (The Oval Attic Window)*, 1916
tr. Mary Ann Caws

*Les Ardoises du toit (Roof Slates)*, 1918
tr. Patricia Terry

Selection from *Étoiles Peintes (Painted Stars)*, 1921
Collected in *Plupart du Temps*
tr. Mary Ann Caws and Patricia Terry

Selection from *Cravates de Chanvre (Ties Made of Hemp)*, 1922
Collected in *Plupart du Temps*
tr. Mary Ann Caws

Selection from *Au Soleil du plafond (The Sun on the Ceiling)*, 1955
tr. Mary Ann Caws and Patricia Terry

Selection from *La Liberté des Mers (The Freedom of the Seas)*, *1960*
tr. Mary Ann Caws and Patricia Terry

*To an enduring dialogue…*

# INTRODUCTION

*My heart is in my
pocket, it is Poems by Pierre Reverdy*

"A Step Away from Them," 1956
—Frank O'Hara

## Pierre Reverdy Now

The importance of Pierre Reverdy, self-effacing though he was in his work as in his life, is nevertheless unquestionable. In 1911, in his influential journal *Nord-Sud* — named after the Paris metro line running North and South, between Montmartre and Montparnasse — he offered a definition of the image crucial to the development of Surrealism and much beyond it. As he wrote, a new and powerful image requires the juxtaposition of two radically distant elements of reality. This was at the heart of the statement made by André Breton, founder of the Surrealist movement, that Reverdy was the most important poet of his generation. Along with Guillaume Apollinaire and Max Jacob, he is often considered at present as representative of Cubism — the literary equivalent of Juan Gris, Pablo Picasso, and Georges Braque — but, as Etienne-Alain Hubert, the editor of his work points out, that falls far short of his essence and importance. In any case, readers of this Black Widow Press collection will find his work so subtle, so varied, and in fact so impersonally intimate, if we can put it like that, that it cannot legitimately be reduced in any way to such a category. We can certainly say that the more one reads Reverdy, the more unlimited is his impact on readers, and, indeed, on writers contemporaneous with and following him.

As well as his considerable influence on Ezra Pound and his followers, Reverdy's influence on more recent American poets has also been considerable. Kenneth Rexroth, in his introduction to his translation of Reverdy's poems, mentions particularly Robert Creeley and Gary Snyder in this context, and cites as another example his own work, defining Reverdy's poetics "as the conscious deliberate dissociation and recombination of elements into a new artistic entity made self-sufficient by its rigorous architecture."

We chose the texts in this collection with two criteria in mind — that they represent Reverdy at his finest, and at the same time read as poems in English. *Les Ardoises du toit (The Roof Slates)*, is given complete, followed by a chronological selection of other poems, ranging over almost half a century, from 1915 to the late 1940s.

## Within the Poems, in Verse and Prose

Reverdy's oddly appealing poetic character can best be judged when his poems in verse and in prose are juxtaposed. If the verse poems, in their layout and their very nature, resemble the poems of no one else, no more do the prose poems fit into any simple scheme of differentiation between "prose" and "verse." The beginning of "Corridor" offers a convenient if fortuitous entrance to both, and to certain problems of their translation:

> There are two of us
>> On the same line where everything
>> follows in night's winding ways

"Two of us" may refer to the poet and a companion, to the poet and his reader, to the poet's own duality, or the reader's. "Everything follows" (*tout se suit*) indicates an unbroken order, as in "one day follows another," or, in its more literally reflexive sense, suggests that everything is in its own order, and that a beginning may be preceded by an ending. The relationship of these various meanings to the "winding ways" either places "the two of us" within the unpredictable mazes of the night, or emphasizes rather a contrast of "lines" with the order of the poem itself predominating. The latter reading will be characteristic of the verse poems, while those in prose tend more to dramatize the poet's difficult experience of darkness. In both orientations the absence of convenient reflexives in English is a serious problem in translating a poet whose constant use of reflexive verbs is symptomatic of introspection in himself and self-awareness in his poems.

In the mobile-like construction of the verse poems the reader's "way" can be complex indeed, involving many reversals in which endings will be seen as beginnings. The prose poems are more direct, whether narrative or descriptive they are poems by virtue of their brevity, the musical quality of the phrases, the density of their language, and their rejection of all that is merely anecdotal in favor of a subjective and dramatic coherence. What is presented is often enigmatic or ambiguous, always extraordinary. In the verse poems, particularly those of *Les Ardoises du toit*, the elements of the poem may be commonplace in themselves; they function aesthetically in juxtaposition.

If we look at a prose poem containing themes that recur in verse, this essential difference will be apparent. In "Strokes and Figures," from a collection published three years before *Les Ardoises du toit*, the world of nature is seen to differ from the urban by its combination of color, light, and clarity, the last two expressed by *éclaircie*, a clearing in the sky, and *clairière*, a clearing in the forest. The imprisoning linear framework of the city has another kind of clarity, that of colorless geometric forms, lines in the service of *bâtisses humaines*, buildings where people live in ugliness. A third domain, the mind of the poet, contains, like the city, "nothing but lines," lines that the poet seeks to "put in order." The poem, however, has a linear order of its own: the clear outline of a formless dilemma.

The opposition between a clearing in nature and clarity in the mind occurs also in "Patience" from *Les Ardoises du toit*. The paratactic structure of the poem, its greater number of elements, and much rarer indications of opinion or emotion, make its "nothing is clear inside my head" very different from the corresponding statement in "Strokes and Figures." One has an impression of what the lack of clarity is in itself, other than simply the contrary of order. In "Patience" the connection between nature and the poet's mind is made through echoes and repetitions. The "clearing" and "nothing is clear" are related by identical sound and opposed meaning; in "Strokes and Figures" color, line, and a lack of order are related by semantic contrast alone.

The discourse in "Strokes and Figures" concerns itself with lines and geometric forms; in "False Portal or Portrait" verbal expression becomes directly spatial: "In this unmoving square," "in the middle," "Tears are rolling through this space." Shapes are also part of the poem's own structure:

> In this unmoving square
> Inside four lines
> A space for the play of white

is opposed to "in the city … the square of the windows." Shapes may materialize through suggestion: the curve of "your cheek," hinting at the roundness of the moon (lune to be read also as *"l'une,"* the one), and anticipating, phonetically and by the transfer of light, the subsequent illumination, *"s'allume."*

"Strokes [traits] and Figures" is the subject; "False Portal" is a "Porte/Trait," a preliminary experience of the poem. The lines surround a mirror that offers a perspective illuminated, not by moonlight, but by the poet ("I am the lamp to guide me"). The mirror-image is both a true representation and a false one, being, as Reverdy might have said, *à l'envers,* in the wrong direction, in re\verse, or inside out — all of which are ways of reading the poem. Had the mirror appeared in a prose poem it might well have represented for the reader simply an element of the description or narration. From the readers' side of the false portal, each of them must perceive the poem as mirroring itself, its portrait, as well as their reading. The mirror is also the mediation between dramatic space and page as well as between poet and reader. The face contemplated thus reveals itself as another face of the text, as the page incorporates all possible reflections.

To this mirror of a poem, the I ("I am the lamp,") and the eye serve as guides. The fact that an eye with a finger on its lid is probably closed indicates the interiority of the vision, a point reinforced by the rhyme *guide/humide.* The door's falsity, an obstacle to progress beyond itself, is thus an opening in another direction.

## Looking again at Pierre Reverdy

Pierre Reverdy, in the early years of the century, was part of the artistic enclave centered around the Bateau-Lavoir on the rue Ravignan in Montmartre that included Guillaume Apollinaire, Max Jacob, Louis Aragon, André Breton, Philippe Soupault and Tristan Tzara, and was enormously admired by the surrealists.

Reverdy, an intensely difficult personality, as if he had been flayed alive — in the fitting description by Etienne-Alain Hubert, the editor of the Flammarion complete two-volume set of Reverdy's poems — adamantly refused to have any chronology attached to his poems and was equally opposed to any biographical details. He would have chosen, as he wrote, to leave behind him just a symbolic portrait, covered with a liquid dust or sea foam, and a voice in suspense. The essential fragments of biography are simply recounted:

Born in Narbonne, in 1889, Reverdy enlisted in the first World War through solidarity with the human condition, and after the vital period of *Nord-Sud* in 1917–18, and encounters with the world of intellectual society, was involved for a time with Catholicism in the early 1920s, and retired, in a voluntary exile, as he put it, only making rare incursions into the world beyond it, to the small monastery town of Solesmes, where he died in 1960.

In this volume, he is represented by work early and late, from the pioneering *Prose Poems* of 1915 and *Roof Slates* of 1918, through *Sun on the Ceiling*, which Reverdy had written in conjunction with Juan Gris's still lifes thirty years earlier, interrupted by the artist's death in 1927 — and only published in 1955.

Unlike any others of his poems, his violently-conceived and brutally-worded, war-haunted poems of 1946–1948, entitled *The Song of the Dead* (illustrated by Picasso, by slashes of red, and reading like a funereal procession toward the final cataclysm, a primitive ossuary, according to François Chapon, his friend in last years), represent a break with his other poems. They were written during the terrible time of the Occupation, with soldiers posted in a part of his house, when he made a "pact with silence," refusing to write or publish, and then in 1946–48 unleashed these songs that had been "repressed in his throat." His final *Freedom of the Seas* of 1960, remarkable for its immense handwriting and Braque's illustrations, published a few weeks before his death, precedes the shifting landscape of his posthumously published epic poem, *Moving Sand*. The crystal drops of *Roof Slates* in 1918 mirror the real snow particles which fell through the ceiling of the almost bare attic in Montmartre where Reverdy met with Louis Aragon, Paul Eluard, and Philippe Soupault in 1919 and 1920, the epoch of the journal *Littérature* (lis-tes-ratures, read your scrapings, went the title). This was Reverdy's own magic domain, full of suggestion and indications as bare as the room: like the surrealist "marvelous," indefinable but somehow precise.

Reverdy, in his terrific and lasting influence not just on surrealism itself, but eventually on the worldwide practice of poetry, represented, said Aragon, the purity of the world. And yet he represented also its misery, reflected in the anger of his eyes, and his gestures: When he had to sell a small Braque painting, he seized it to kiss it farewell, to the astonishment of the wealthy purchaser. His apparent self-renunciation, his voluntary refusal to appear in his texts, generally governed by the impersonal "on," runs counter to the overwhelming fact: poetry *was* emotion for him, as he put it, and his interior drama infuses it even as he seems absent from its surface. Or almost.

In 1926, after a period of intense involvement with Catholicism and association with Jacques and Raissa Maritain, he went into voluntary exile from the world, as he put it in his journal, near the monastery of Solesmes, with his wife, only making rare expeditions to the capital... He was to live estranged from society and from his faith, in the long run. A poem for his wife finds them at the edge of a well, recounting how hard it was "to live/Our painful existence" and awaiting the night: handwritten on the page are the lines:

> The lamp light is giving out
>> It's getting late.

Until his death in 1960 in Solesmes, nothing of the lived factual was to penetrate the poetic domain, conceived as pure emotion: no biographical or chronological intrusion that would fix the moment. The poems are set in an uncertain time and place, just a vibration beyond the specific into the universal. "I am alone…Alone…" in some pure prideful place, where the details are suffered, but only burst into cruel expression in the *Song of the Dead*, a cosmic lament for all and everything.

The "shifting landscape" of his posthumously published *Moving Sand* perfectly seizes his kind of poetry, as his editor Etienne-Alain Hubert puts it, "outside of time outside of history, outside of geography…in an eternal actuality." The strength of this two-person selection and translation of Reverdy's poetry is the dialogic aspect of the voices responding to his interior voice, often muted, sometimes harsh, always worth a time of listening and answering, in a shifting landscape of interiorized poetry. That is the purpose of this book, in which the translations are also — overall — by "the two of us."

*—Mary Ann Caws and Patricia Terry*

## Le livre de mon bord / My Notebook: Notes 1930–1936

The numbers refer to the pages in the Flammarion edition of *Pierre Reverdy: Oeuvres complètes*, tome II

p. 24   We should take life the way we sit down to dinner — with the simple idea of coming to the end having lost any desire to live or to eat.

p. 37   Elegant, that is, detached.

p. 38   To be nothing is to be master of everything. But that depends on what those who claim not to need anything are content with. The only thing we really need is not to need.

p. 49   It's through this desperate need of fulfillment, specific to human beings, that what is called the soul can most easily be defined — a desire never fully achieved. So the soul is a lack, an emptiness that nothing tangible or definable can ever satisfy.

p. 84   Strength is central — but inertia, alas, is too.

p. 89   If we were ever satisfied by something, it would more likely be by little than by a lot.

p. 91   We all know how things happen. You put one foot in front of the other, the way you always do, and… an accident happens. Yesterday, it was a pleasant walk, today, an accident.

p. 95   A lot of insensitivity may look like courage.

p. 98   Has there ever been any greater example of human self-esteem than to believe us worthy of God?

p. 98   Those people who are always so self-possessed, you can be sure that they love nothing or anyone too much.

p. 100  With our interior and everyone else's façade, we build rather luxurious houses.

p. 645  The sailboat is in the harbor. But there are no sails. Instead of sails, there is smoke. It's the smoke which attracts or repels us, and we have only one desire left, one need, one anguish — to unfurl. How can the smoke which attracts or repels us help us? It's about leaving and starting down the trembling gangplank.

p. 648  What defines us is our inexplicable need for the marvelous. And that's what's most crucial about our divorce from nature. We don't believe in miracles anymore — that's obvious. But the miracles we don't believe in anymore are nothing compared to those which all of us keep way down inside and that our imagination is constantly offering us.

p. 652  The mind created time and finds it long. Since it didn't create life, it always finds it a bit short.

p. 653  I wanted intelligence to serve talent. Now I want talent to serve intelligence. Nothing is more exalting than giving intelligence its due, so that it is alive and dominant.

p. 654  We spend part of our lives seeing ourselves powerful and generous, then, when the dream has lost a bit of its enthusiasm, we have a hard time restraining the excessive impulses of this artificial character, impulses which would like to be reality.

p. 655  One can be very accomplished and just as weak, for strength doesn't come so much from the quantity of gifts as from their balance.

p. 655  Someone I know wishes to have a mind as great and subtle as his body is short and thick.

p. 655  We shouldn't always wait to be in agreement with the grandeur and nobility of others to find them good company. In gears there is the prong — but you need the empty space also.

p. 655   Nature does things too well, not having put a pen in our hands.

p. 656   The thick substance of common sense that reassures and weighs down.

p. 657   We talk to ourselves but we don't write to ourselves unless we are crazy. We write for other people, but we don't know exactly for whom. Aren't we rather crazy?

p. 658   About the only things that we consider truly evil are those we feel obliged to hide.

p. 658   When they reach a certain age, artists have much more need of admirers than of friends.

p. 658   As human beings, we are superior to animals — but not as animals.

*Tr. Mary Ann Caws and Patricia Terry*

Selection from

*Poèmes en Prose
(Prose Poems)*
1915

Translated by Mary Ann Caws

# PREFACE TO PROSE POEMS

*Real poetry is a gesture that counts. (This Emotion Called Poetry)*

## Choice and Metapoetic

The subjects treated in this range of prose poems are few; they have been simply and openly chosen according to a subjective taste, but in the belief that they are also representative. They are situated in a certain landscape that we come to recognize, and that will not easily be forgotten, composed as it is of certain highly charged images and figures, traversed as it is by certain lines and strokes. These meditations on the poetic self, highly aware of its own creative oddness and its own peculiar genius, choose their setting and, on the whole, construct it as surroundings for the self. Regardless of the date of the text, this self is unmistakable: many of the poems, from early to late, illustrate above all an exacerbated reticence, as in the title given to one of the Prose Poems of 1915: "Timidity." It seems only fitting that such a narrator should have his hat knocked off by the wind… But the extraordinarily acute perception of the stranger aspects of the lonely mind and of the obsessions governing it account for many of the less common aspects of Reverdy's style.

May not, in fact, the hypertense trouble of the underlying text as it clashes with the calmer surface — that surface that keeps a very low profile — be considered to depend on precisely this oddity of personality? May not, moreover, what we would unquestionably recognize as Reverdy's extraordinary poetic sensitivity be intimately involved in his excruciating nervousness? I think we might understand his as a nervous perception, which should be celebrated as such, quite on the other side of the famous "monotony." ("I may be boring," said André Breton, "but Pierre Reverdy is still more boring than I am.") The nuanced perception demanded of the reader is here interior to the design and the structure of the poems, and what might have appeared monotonous in them turns out — once seen from the inside — to be full of differentiation, color, and contrast.

In the prose poems exactly these nuances are clear: a development of the range and sort of interior perception is noticeable within them, even in their titles, from the peculiarly neutral titles of the *Prose Poems* (1915) and the *Some*

*Poems* (1916) on to the visions already framed by the title that gives the perspective from which they look, these poems of *The Oval Attic Window* (1916), as we have translated the *Lucarne ovale*. That this *Lucarne ovale* can just as well be a skylight as a dormer or attic-window links the point of the viewer's vision, which is to say, his viewpoint, also to *Les Ardoises du toit* and to the *(Étoiles peintes) Painted Stars* (1921), even in some sense to the *Glass Puddles* (1929), since these are all constructions made between the sky in its brilliance and human vision or artifice: drops in the gutter of the roof, stars caught in the mirror of a water as in a glass, or painted, quite simply, upon a windowpane. And all these senses are held, too, in the clear ambiguities of the sounds as of the sight. Held, then, in a glass, as in the *Plein verre* or *Full Glass* of a collection of poems from 1940, or in a mirror, that *verre* of the *Flaques de verre* where the stillness of the puddles turns them into a capturing surface, or then, within a verse, that *vers* echoing in all the titles of these conscious poems about poetry. Metapoetic, they are undeniably that: and yet their fresh quality as picture is maintained, as in the later *Bois vert* or *Green Wood* (1946–49), where the same sound *(vers/verre)* as that capturing the glass, the mirror, and the poem, now brings out the density of the fullest cluster of sense and sound, each meaning triggering the reader's retrospective or prospective reading of the others. An extensive experience facilitates this reaction. On the other side of the crystalline imagery, the harshness of *Ferraille (Scrap Iron)*, 1937, brings out the alternate intelligence of the poet's *faire*, his making, in its alliance with the *fer* or iron, replacing and yet echoing in its own rhyme the *verre/vert*. As if Reverdy were indeed obsessed with that rhyme, the last collection of his poems, *The Freedom of the Seas (La Liberté des mers)* from 1959, retains the *-er,* the sea of the final syllable holding in itself both the *verre* in its glassiness and the *fer* in its construction.

Now if we consider that single case of triple and quadruple meaning as the sound is charged with its multiplicity, and consider also the frequency of this occurrence, each reader may well wonder to what extent other interpretations should be conjured up within the poems, whether or not Reverdy's intentions are taken into account. He himself, in an essay of 1938, semi-ironically called "To Have Done with Poetry," says the following: "If poetry makes too many compromises with the ear, it does not reach the mind — if it weighs on the mind, it has lost all its wing-feathers. The ear is the keyhole opening onto the heart" (*This Emotion*, p. 138). So both the glass *(verre)* and the line *(vers)* and the freshness of the green *(vert)* may be included in the mind, in its own opening upon the heart. The summit poem of *Flaques de verre* is called, appropriately, "The Head Filled with Beauty," and it links the lines or vers with the others beyond them, to which it refers, in the built-in library of intertextual references; the poet here addresses, as it were, the poetry directly, and in an accumulating crescendo:

> You, gentleness and hatred — horizon chipped away, pure line of indifference and oblivion. You, this morning, totally alone, in order, calm, and universal revolution. You, diamond nail. You, purity, dazzling swivel of the ebb and flow of my thought in the lines of the world.
> (pp. 134-5)

Throughout these poems, what strikes the alerted reader even more than the individual themes may well be the essentially metapoetic quality of these texts, many of which refer mainly to their own being as texts: thus the continued emphasis on windows and door, on frames and curtains and edges, rims of a glass, the *bords* or borders of riverbanks or ravines, and the distinctions between light and shadow, lamps and what they reflect upon. These images can all be seen, I think, as the indications of a particular interest in the devices through or by which vision is itself bordered: an oval holds a face, as in "Soul and Body Superposed," or a portrait is framed by a window in a great number of poems: "A Mediocre Appearance," "Civil," "Trips Too Long," "Another Face," "At the Moment of the Banquet," "Afternoon," "Outside," among others.

Of all the devices, the most emblematic or self-sufficient — needing no interpretation beyond itself — is perhaps that of the finger and the hands, to which attention is drawn over and over. In the poem "When One is Not of This World," whose title may already be seen as a distancing of the poet from those who are of another calling — whose hands would undoubtedly be less in evidence — fingers trace upon a tablecloth an undecipherable name in large black letters, whereas in the poems of the last collection fingers are flung to the ceiling at the same moment that a spider is seen to be busily and vainly spinning, giving the title "The Web" to the poem, whose own web neatly links one "useless" gesture to another. (The poem is reminiscent of an earlier one, where hands are outstretched under a lamp; in another of the poems in *The Freedom of the Seas*, "The Mind Outside," hands are once more stretched out under the lamp, and a pen scratches late across a page. Elsewhere, white hands flutter, and everywhere, the mind grapples with its own self-mockery and with "The Luck of Words," as if it were some card game whose images captured the Cubist eye, whose luck involved us all, and poetry. We have only to note how many of the texts are called by such titles: "The Poets," "The Word," "The Luck of Words," "Mirror of Ink," to support the easily supported hypothesis that words, hands, and eyes, are all dissociated from ordinary language, severed from the matter of ordinary bodies and visions — as in the image from "The Poets," with severed hands lit under the lamp. Stressed, exalted in their very separation, these few images are charged now with special significance, emblematized in the poetry centered upon itself. This is of course a widespread notion, but Reverdy's "Chambre noire," or darkroom, with its claustrophobic atmosphere, impressive to the reader, helps to create the illusion that the self-reference is in this case especially acute.

## A Moody Line

> In my head, lines, nothing but lines;
> if only I could make some order of them.
> (Strokes and Figures)

As for the ambiance of the poems, the figures betraying it are to be read in their own context, and total submersion in Reverdy's universe is preferable to occasional plunges to its depths. The atmosphere tends toward the gloomy: after an exaltation of action, the closure is often associated with deception. For example, in "After the Ball," dancers spin about and then the lamps are extinguished, so that the erstwhile dancer is alone in the cold, leaving the impression that something is missing. The road is often blocked ("Soul and Body Superposed"), the curtains are often drawn to close off the poem at the end of a spectacle, or the light goes out ("The Ridiculous Bodies of the Minds"), or the day ends ("Light"); the fields are most probably devastated ("Flames"), the rain most probably icy, the wall soaked or dirtied, the dress sodden, the sky gray, and the very air may well be blue-black and sore, as in the title "The Bruised Air." Rugs are discolored ("Carnival") as is the flag whose symbol seems to wear off ("Battle"), a white glove is faded ("Brief Life") — in short, the physical universe is usually leaden and the human, fatigued ("Reality of Shadows" and passim). Thoughts will most likely be "low" or "lowly"; a child is starving, soldiers are afflicted, like poets, with nightmares.

But a mud puddle will suffice to capture the spectacle and the light of a universe, here as in Rimbaud's "Drunken Boat" or in the poetry of Yves Bonnefoy, where language serves in just this manner:

Les mots comme le ciel,

Infini,

Mais tout entier soudain dans la flaque brève.


(The words like the sky,

Infinite,

But entire suddenly in the brief puddle.)

—In the Threshold's Lure


The *Glass Puddles*, then, are a mirror for poetic reflection: "To Each His Share" explains how such a water is sufficient for a strange fisherman-like poet, who will not, as does another fisherman, scoop gold pieces whose gleam will be extinguished in a closed basket — who will not content himself, then, with the reflection of mere wealth, but rather, will dangle the line into the stars themselves as they shine within the water, these illusions being the matter for real fishing, for real poets:

This water, having come from the sky, was filled with stars.

And the stars are no less real there than the diamonds caught in the gutter of the roof, the diamond nail caught in the glass of some great poem, like a painted star of the *Etoiles peintes;* for in that puddle there is to be found all *The Freedom of the Seas*.


## Character and Some Clarifications

Reverdy's singular character certainly informed his singular genius. Despite his disinclination to have a chronological sweep to his poetry — preferring, as he did, to set a distance between his personal life and his published work — a few things seem nonetheless clear about his personality as it relates to his writings.

First of all, I would put the tension between his genuine desire for obscurity as expressed in one of his prayers, as quoted by a close friend:

"Please make certain, Lord, that I will remain an unknown poet"[1] and his disappointment over feeling forgotten after the epoch of the cubist journal *Nord-Sud*, 1916–1917. In fact, his choice of the prose poem was related to this great disillusion. As Etienne-Alain Hubert puts it in his definitive edition of Reverdy's work, this form was that in which "the being already torn and wounded that he was believed he could keep a distance between the felt and the written…the harsh emergency of the first person singular to recount in turn the sometimes bitter lucidity of the interior disaster: 'Je suis un témoignage fendu de la tête aux pieds.' (I am a witness split from my head to my feet.")[2]

And the unquestionable prickliness of his poems — in verse and prose — betrays the character marked by "the combative impulse of Reverdy, a being as unmanageable in his relation to others as with himself."[3] After his retreat to Solesmes in 1926, Reverdy marked his unease with the institution of religion and the display of conversions in this period, remarking on his prolonged independence: "Je ne suis lié à rien ni à personne" (I am linked to nothing and no one) and commenting on his option of exile: "This step toward God was a step of retreat from life."

As he remarked later, on this retreat: "What an intellectual adventure is living among four walls. Everything lost in expansion gains in density. The being is dilated and evaporates in freedom, it concentrates and hardens itself in prison."[4] This was what he conceived of as the "concentration of personality" after which he sought.

A few clarifications about some of the works from which selections appear here should prove useful to the reader. All appear in the edition of Reverdy's complete works as edited by Etienne-Alain Hubert and published in 2010. The nine poems of *Bois vert* (of which one has been selected, and an odd poem it is!) were added at the last minute to the volume of *Main d'oeuvre* in order to display the fact that Reverdy was writing "avant-garde" material earlier than had been thought — as early as Paul Eluard, for example, with whom there was a certain rivalry. The title of *Sources du vent* was originally *Flammes*, then *Source du vent*, before the final title: *Sources du vent*. The importance of the plural title, already occurring in *Les Ardoises du toit* and then recurring in the prose poems of *Flaques de verre*, related in the latter to a form resembling "transparent fragments shining on the ground which receives them when they fall."[5]

The form of fragments or notes is found particularly in *Le Gant de crin* (following on his baptism in May of 1921 and his retreat to the Abbaye of Solesmes, and relating to the horsehair glove, with which God treats his friends, according to the author, a volume Reverdy finally thought little of ), and then in *Le Livre de mon bord* (selections quoted here), as well as in *En vrac*. This form, fragmentary and revelatory of highly differing moods, was particularly congenial to him:

> I don't think, I take notes,

and then:

> Incapable of reasoning, I restricted myself
> to taking notes.[6]

The aphoristic style common to Valéry, whose theoretical writings he much admired, and Nietzsche, whose works he read in 1929–1930, struck him "like a rubdown with a fistful of snow"[6] What he especially disliked was the journal or the diary (about Gide's *Journal,* he noted: "I have a horror of the diary that a writer expends little upon as the most precious and insidious of books")[7] so his *Livre de mon bord,* dating from the year 1936 when he traveled to Greece, was a reworking of previous notes. Yet he worried about this form also, as he noted to himself in 1932: "I think too much about form — I am not sincere — I am too preoccupied with the effect. I don't give myself over — I want to convince and impress."

## Interior Perception and the Self of Poetry

> — What was the major encounter of your life? (question asked
> in 1934 for the journal *Minotaure*)

> — The only one, capital and so obviously necessary ... that which
> I believe I had with myself, which will never end.

> (*This Emotion,* p. 175)

Nowhere are Reverdy's aesthetics better summed up than in the essays grouped under the title *This Emotion Called Poetry: Writings on Poetry 1930–1960,* with the invaluable notes and commentaries furnished, as for all the Flammarion editions, by Etienne-Alain Hubert: this is the collection whose ancestor is the volume of essays on art and poetry collected in *Nord-Sud: Self-Defense* ... Here, as always, the poet's attitude is a self-sufficient one: "to create an aesthetic work made of one's own means, a particular emotion that the things of nature, in their own situation, are not able to provoke in man." The explicit goal is the augmentation of being that a poem expresses and maintains: the love of the real through the book is along Mallarmé's lines, and in his line of sight; toward the self, the self struggles, through a vocabulary deliberately narrowed and vision in its self-enforced closure, masking and shutting off. (Seen in this light, the ubiquitous references to masks and masking are part of a whole attitude and concern, and not just the bizarre obsession of some psychotic writer.)

This volume also, being only a translation and secondhand representation, is limited by its words and by their weakness, and dependent on the sensitivity that it is our aim to develop, in spite of and because of the very closure of the "dark room" that Reverdy uses so often as the image of the development of poetry. The sensitivity is a quiet one. It is not here a question of Rimbaldian dazzle in illumination, of Mallarméan complexity in its exhilaration, or of the monumental subtlety and the subtle monumentality of René Char, but rather of some summit within the poetic being — some other "Head Filled with Beauty" of an almost imperceptible kind, visible in any case only after the reading of a great deal of this poetry. Toward this perception Reverdy's reader may move, conscious that Reverdy's own manner is already a refusal of flashiness or outward drama. This is, and here the reader must share Reverdy's own faith, a work with delayed action, an *"Oeuvre à retardement"* (*This Emotion*, p. 112), a work whose beauty and force are revealed

> very slowly, by successive generations and for eminently contradictory reasons, that is to say, works holding in their net enough mystery to be only with great difficulty accessible to the simple watchers of the present — in brief, those works including between their visible constitutive elements enough white space, enough margin, so that succeeding generations can come to deposit in them, never weakening or profoundly altering the purity and value of their original structure, as much and even more substance than they could have gotten themselves. For in a work which lasts without aging, which grows while it lasts, all those who claim to love it, to understand it, to comment upon it, to spread it by

amplifying it with a legend, even one which deforms it
most of the time, all these collaborate. (*This Emotion,*
pp. 112–113)

The present work, which desires to be a faithful reflection of and upon Reverdy's
own work, tries neither to spread a legend nor to make an extensive commentary,
but simply to participate, insofar as possible, in its own interior sensitivity.

*—Mary Ann Caws*

[1]    Quoted in Axel Madsen, *Biography of Coco Chanel,* Bloomsbury, 1990, p. 197.
[2]    Pierre Reverdy, *Oeuvres complètes,* Paris: Flammarion, 2010, Tome II, p. 1497.
[3]    *Ibid,* p. 1489.
[4]    *Ibid,* p. 1497, 1508.
[5]    *Ibid,* p. 1507.
[6]    *Ibid,* p. 1498, 1517.
[7]    *Ibid,* pp. 1509–1510.

## FÉTICHE

Petite poupée, marionnette porte-bonheur, elle se débat à ma fenêtre, au gré du vent. La pluie a mouillé sa robe, sa figure et ses mains qui déteignent. Elle a même perdu une jambe. Mais sa bague reste, et, avec elle, son pouvoir. L'hiver elle frappe à la vitre de son petit pied chaussé de bleu et danse, danse de joie, de froid pour réchauffer son cœur, son cœur de bois porte-bonheur. La nuit, elle lève ses bras suppliants vers les étoiles.

## LE VENT ET L'ESPRIT

C'est une étonnante chimère. La tête, plus haut que cet étage, se place entre les deux fils de fer et se cale et se tient; rien ne bouge.

La tête inconnue parle et je ne comprends aucun mot, je n'entends aucun son — bas contre terre. Je suis toujours sur le trottoir d'en face et je regarde; je regarde les mots qu'emporte le vent; les mots qu'il va jeter plus loin. La tête parle et je n'entends rien, le vent disperse tout.

O grand vent, moqueur ou lugubre, j'ai souhaité ta mort. Et je perds mon chapeau que tu m'as pris aussi. Je n'ai plus rien; mais ma haine dure, hélas plus que toi-même.

## HIVER

À travers la pluie dense et glacée de ce soir-là où le boulevard s'éclaire, un petit homme noir au visage bleu. Est-ce de froid? Est-ce du feu interne qu'allume l'alcool?

Mais ses souliers trop grands sont pleins d'eau et il tourne autour des réverbères. C'est la joie et la pitié des filles. Quelle lourde émotion! Qui voudra l'enlever?

O monde sans abri qui vas ce dur chemin et qui t'en moques, je ne te comprends pas. J'aime la tièdeur, le confort, et la quiétude.

O monde qui les méprises, tu me fais peur!

## FETISH

Tiny doll and marionette for a charm, thrashing about at my window by the will of the wind. Rain has dampened her dress, her face, and her hands whose color is fading. She has even lost a leg. But her ring remains and with it, her power. In wintertime, she raps against the windowpane with her little blue-shod foot and dances, dances for joy. With cold to warm up her heart, her charmed-wood heart. Nightly, she lifts her arms in supplication toward the stars.


## THE WIND AND THE SPIRIT

An astonishing chimera. The head, higher than this room, fits between the two wires, settles, and is still: nothing moves.

The unknown head speaks and I grasp not a word, hear not a sound — low as the earth. I am still on the sidewalk opposite and I am looking, looking at the words the wind carries off, the words it will later cast away. The head speaks and I hear nothing, the wind disperses everything.

Oh great wind, mocking or lugubrious. I have longed for your death. Deprived of my hat you've snatched from me too. I have nothing any longer; but my hatred endures, alas, longer than you.


## WINTER

Through the dense and icy rain of that evening when the boulevard lights up, a small black man with a face gone blue. From the cold? Or the internal blaze drink has kindled?

But his shoes, too large for him, are water-logged, and he circles around the street lamps. He's the joy and the pity of the whores. What a weight of feeling! Who'd agree to remove it?

Oh shelterless world along this harsh path, uncaring, I don't understand you. I like things tepid, comfortable, and tranquil.

Oh world disdaining these things, you frighten me.

## HÔTELS

Dans une singulière détresse d'or j'attends, passé minuit, que vienne l'heure propice à toutes les défenses contre les éléments. Je vais passer devant l'ennemi, redoutable plus que la pluie, plus que le froid. Il dort et ma main tremble. Une petite arme me suffira, mais avec ce terrible bruit dans la serrure et de la porte, je vais être assailli d'horribles cauchemars.

Au matin nouveau, départ à pas de chat. C'est un autre soupir et la rue me devient moins hostile; mais quand viendront, enfin, la délivrance et le repos tranquille? Cependant je me souviens d'avoir dormi dans un lit plus doux dressé pour moi.

Il n'en reste plus que les rêves.

## CARNAVAL

Les tapis fortement secoués laissaient des signes entre les arbres. On les avait déteints avec les pieds.

Sur les quais, avec un regard attendri, les têtes se tournaient, mais les passants gardaient leur masque.

Toute la perspective se bariolait en tapis déteints ou plus riches et parfois on entendait des cris qui proclamaient la honte de ceux qu'on attaquait. Le soir. la lumière et les ombres se battent. Masquée, toute la haine se choque et le mieux caché devient le plus hardi.

C'est un grand divertissement général, un jeu et ce jeu c'est encore une lutte.

## HOTELS

In an odd golden distress I have been waiting, past midnight, for the time propitious for all possible defenses against the elements. I shall pass before the enemy, more to be feared than rain, more than cold. He sleeps and my hand trembles. A small weapon will suffice, but with this terrible noise in the keyhole and at the door, I shall be prey to horrendous nightmares.

In the fresh morning, departure quiet as a cat. Another sigh and the street becomes less hostile for me; but when will I have deliverance and peaceful rest? However I remember having slept in a softer bed made up for me.

Of it only dreams remain.


## CARNIVAL

The rugs briskly shaken out left signs between the trees. Feet had discolored them.

On the wharfs, the heads turned, tenderness in their gaze, but the passersby kept their masks.

The whole perspective turned multi-striped in rugs discolored or richer, and sometimes cries announced the shame of those attacked. In the evening, light and the shadows struggle. Masked, the totality of hatred collides and the most cleverly hidden becomes the most daring.

A great general diversion, a game and this game is still a struggle.

## LES POÈTES

Sa tête s'abritait craintivement sous l'abat-jour de la lampe. Il est vert et ses yeux sont rouges. Il y a un musicien qui ne bouge pas. Il dort; ses mains coupées jouent du violon pour lui faire oublier sa misère.

Un escalier qui ne conduit nulle part grimpe autour de la maison. Il n'y a, d'ailleurs, ni portes ni fenêtres. On voit sur le toit s'agiter des ombres qui se précipitent dans le vide. Elles tombent une à une et ne se tuent pas. Vite par l'escalier elles remontent et recommencent, éternellement charmées par le musicien qui joue toujours du violon avec ses mains qui ne l'écoutent pas.


## TRAITS ET FIGURES

Une éclaircie avec du bleu dans le ciel; dans la forêt des clairières toutes vertes; mais dans la ville où le dessin nous emprisonne, l'arc de cercle du porche, les carrés des fenêtres, les losanges des toits.

Des lignes, rien que des lignes, pour la commodité des bâtisses humaines.

Dans ma tête des lignes, rien que des lignes; si je pouvais y mettre un peu d'ordre seulement.


## A L'AUBE

Dans mon rêve la tête d'un enfant était au centre.

Si les nuages s'accumulent sur ton toit et que la pluie t'épargne garderas-tu le secret de ce double miracle?

Mais aucune voix ne t'appelle. Si tu te lèves, pieds nus, tu prendras mal. Où irais-tu d'ailleurs, à travers ces ravins de lumières?

L'édredon gardait le silence; les jambes repliées sous lui il marche sur ses ailes et sort. C'était un ange et le matin plus blanc qui se levait.

## THE POETS

His head took shelter fearfully under the lampshade. It is green, his eyes red. There is a musician who does not move. He sleeps: his severed hands play the violin to help him forget his misery.

A staircase leading nowhere climbs round the house. Nor are there any doors or windows. On the roof shadows can be seen shifting about and hurtling into emptiness. One by one they fall, unharmed. Quickly they move back up the stairs and start again, eternally charmed by the violinist still playing, his hands not listening.

## STROKES AND FIGURES

A bluetinged clearing in the sky; in the forest, clearings quite green; but in the town where pattern imprisons us, the arch of the porch circle, the squares of windows, the diamonds of the roofs.

Lines, nothing but lines, for the convenience of human buildings.

In my head lines, nothing but lines; if only I could make some order of them.

## AT DAWN

In my dream a child's bed was at the center.

If the clouds accumulate on your roof and the rain spares you, will you keep the secret of this double miracle?

But no voice calls you. If you rise barefooted, you will catch a cold. Where would you go anyway, across these ravines of lights?

The eiderdown kept still. His legs folded under him, he walks on his wings and departs, an angel and the whiter morn arising.

## INCOGNITO

Une première fois sa canne tombe et il remonte sur le trottoir.

La jambe droite s'écarte de la ligne du triangle et, de dos, son âge l'accompagne. Serait-il si vieux?

Son temps se passe à déjouer la stratégie des filles. Au carrefour il s'évanouit dans l'ombre et la voiture l'emporte.

C'était peut-être un roi, déguisé en vieillard timide et malheureux.


## LE VOYAGEUR ET SON OMBRE

Il faisait si chaud qu'il laissait au courant de la route tous ses vêtements un à un. Il les laissait accrochés aux buissons. Et, quand il fut nu, il s'approchait déjà de la ville. Une honte immense s'empara de lui et l'empêcha d'entrer. Il était nu et comment ne pas attirer les regards?

Alors il contourna la ville et entra par la porte opposée. Il avait pris la place de son ombre qui, passant la première, le protégeait.


## L'AIR MEURTRI

Il fait si chaud que l'air vibre et que tout bruit devient assourdissant. Des meutes de chiens féroces aboient. Par les fenêtres ouvertes, les cris des femmes rivalisent avec cette fanfare barbare.

Le froid a de la peine à geler ces paroles. Si les oiseaux se taisaient, si les femmes se taisaient, si les chiens étaient morts … Un moment les jardins sont calmes et tout s'endort; mais bientôt le terrible bruit recommence. Ce sont les appels du soleil et chacun y répond avec exubérance. Quelques êtres muets qu'on accable ne peuvent protester ni se venger. Le bruit souverain les opprime.

Dans les fumées, par-dessus les toits qui s'en préservent seuls, j'aurais fait tournoyer ma tête comme un grelot sans pois au bout d'une ficelle. La vitesse ouatée jusqu'aux nuages et permettre au ruisseau de murmurer tout seul!

Le ciel est descendu, on a refermé les fenêtres et les bouches sont closes. Après la chute des feuilles les oiseaux même n'osent plus gazouiller. Il fait si froid.

L'hiver c'est l'intervalle du silence.

## INCOGNITO

For the first time his cane falls and he climbs back up on the sidewalk.

The right leg leaves the triangle's line, and from behind, his age moves along with him. Could he be so old?

His time is spent foiling the strategy of the girls. At the crossroads he faints in the shadow and the coach bears him away.

Perhaps he was a king, disguised as an old man, timid and unhappy.


## THE VOYAGER AND HIS SHADOW

It was so hot that he shed his clothes one by one along the road. He left them hanging on the shrubs. And when he was naked, he was already nearing the town. An immense shame came over him and kept him from entering. He was naked, and how could he help being stared at?

Then he went round the town and entered by the opposite gate. He had taken the place of his shadow which, going first, protected him.


## THE BRUISED AIR

It is so hot that the air vibrates and any noise deafens. Hordes of ferocious dogs are barking. Through the open windows, the cries of women vie with this barbaric fanfare.

The cold can scarcely freeze these words. If birds kept silent, if women hushed, if dogs were dead … For a moment, the gardens are calm and all drifts back to sleep; but soon the fearful noise begins once more … These are the summons of the sun and everyone answers with exuberance. Some mute and burdened beings can neither protest nor avenge themselves. The noise in its dominance oppresses them.

In the smoke above the roofs which alone stay out of the din, I would have had my head spin about like the clapper of the empty sleighbell. Muffled speed up to the clouds and let the stream murmur all alone!

The heavens descended, the windows have been closed again, and the mouths also. After the fall of leaves even the birds dare not chirp. It is so cold.

Winter is the interval of silence.

## LA REPASSEUSE

Autrefois ses mains faisaient des taches roses sur le linge éclatant qu'elle repassait. Mais dans la boutique où le poêle est trop rouge son sang s'est peu à peu évaporé. Elle devient de plus en plus blanche et dans la vapeur qui monte on la distingue à peine au milieu des vagues luisantes des dentelles.

Ses cheveux blonds flottent dans l'air en boucles de rayons et le fer continue sa route en soulevant du linge des nuages — et autour de la table son âme qui résiste encore, son âme de repasseuse court et plie comme le linge en fredonnant une chanson — sans que personne y prenne garde.

## UNE APPARENCE MÉDIOCRE

Le train siffle et repart dans la fumée qui se fond au ciel bas.

C'est un long convoi de larmes et sur chaque quai où l'on se  sépare de nouveaux bras agitent des mouchoirs. Mais celui-là est seul et ses lunettes se ternissent des larmes des autres ou de la pluie qui fouette la vitre où il colle son nez. Il n'a quitté personne et nul ne l'attendra à la gare où il va descendre.

D'ailleurs il ne raconte pas ses voyages, il ne sait pas décrire les pays qu'il a vus. Il n'a rien vu peut-être, et quand on le regarde, de peur qu'on l'interroge, il baisse les yeux ou les lève vers le ciel où d'autres nuages se fondent. A l'arrivée, sans expression de joie ou d'impatience, il part, seul dans la nuit, et, sous les becs de gaz qui l'éclairent par intervalles, on le voit disparaître, sa petite valise à la main. Il est seul, on le croit seul. Pourtant quelque chose le suit ou peut-être quelqu'un dans la forme étrange de son ombre.

## THE WOMAN IRONING

Once her hands used to make rose-colored spots on the gleaming linen she ironed. But in the shop where the stove is too hot her blood has evaporated little by little. She becomes whiter and whiter and in the rising steam you can barely make her out among the lace in its shiny undulations.

Her blonde hair floats in the air in radiant curls and the iron continues its path, raising clouds from the linen — and around the table her soul still resisting, her ironer's soul runs about and is pleated like the linen humming a song — without anyone noticing.

## A MEDIOCRE APPEARANCE

The train whistles and sets off again in the smoke melting in the low sky.

Tears in a long convoy and on each track where people part, other arms wave handkerchiefs. But that one is alone and his glasses mist with others' tears or with the rain lashing the windowpane where his nose presses. He has left no one and will be met by no one at the station.

Nor does he tell about his trips, unable to describe the countries he has seen. Perhaps he has seen nothing and when he is looked at, fearful lest he be asked a question, he lowers his eyes or raises them toward the sky where other clouds are melting. At his arrival, with no expression of joy or impatience, he sets off alone in the night, and under the gas lamps lighting him now and again, he is seen disappearing, his small suitcase in his hand. He is alone, seems to be alone. Still, something is following him or perhaps someone in the strange form of his shadow.

## L'INTRUS

Entre les 4 murs de cette salle basse se mouvaient des esprits obscurs et d'autres extrêmement légers et lumineux.

Un homme presque nu entra au milieu de ces toiles et dans ces étendues de glace et de désert.

Il entraînait une caravane en désordre et marchait seul. Une voix qui venait d'ailleurs faisait tinter à nos oreilles un son nouveau. Mais dans ce mélange de capes et d'épées, de chansons et de cris, il régnait un air de carnival — il y manquait surtout la grâce avec l'esprit.

Un monde très ancien tournoyait dans nos têtes et l'on attendait le moment où tout allait tomber.

Mais, dehors, au lieu d'un clair de lune sur un fond de décor — on trouvait un temps gris où manœuvraient les machines hurlantes dissipant le malaise. Dans la rue, nous avions retrouvé la foule et notre siècle. Mais tous ces esprits obscurs ou lumineux, légers et lourds, et l'homme nu de quelle époque étaient-ils descendus ce soir-là?


## BELLE ÉTOILE

J'aurai peut-être perdu la clé, et tout le monde rit autour de moi et chacun me montre une clé énorme pendue à son cou.

Je suis le seul à ne rien avoir pour entrer quelque part. Ils ont tous disparu et les portes closes laissent la rue plus triste. Personne. Je frapperai partout.

Des injures jaillissent des fenêtres et je m'éloigne.

Alors un peu plus loin que la ville, au bord d'une rivière et d'un bois, j'ai trouvé une porte. Une simple porte à claire-voie et sans serrure. Je me suis mis derrière et, sous la nuit qui n'a pas de fenêtres mais de larges rideaux, entre la forêt et la rivière qui me protègent, j'ai pu dormir.

## THE INTRUDER

Between the 4 walls of this low room, somber spirits wandered, and others extremely light and luminous.

A man almost naked entered amid these canvasses and in these stretches of ice and desert.

With him he brought a caravan of disorder and walked alone. A voice which came from elsewhere rang a new sound in our ears. But in this mixture of capes and swords, of songs and shouts, a carnival air reigned — above all grace was missing, and wit.

An ancient world spun about in our heads and we awaited the moment when everything would collapse.

But outside, instead of moonlight on a theatre backdrop, there was a gray weather, where shrieking machines were to dissipate anxiety. In the street we had found the crowd once more and our own century. But from what epoch had there come all these somber or luminous spirits, light and heavy, and the naked man that evening?

## UNDER THE STARS

I have in all likelihood lost the key and everyone laughs all about me, each one showing me a mammoth key hung about his neck.

I am the only one with no place to enter. They have all disappeared and the closed doors leave the street sadder. No one. I shall knock everywhere.

Insults lash forth from windows and I go on.

Then a way past the town, at the edge of a river and a wood, I found a door. A simple wicket gate and no lock. I placed myself behind it and, under the night with no windows but wide curtains, between the forest and the river protecting me, I could sleep.

## CIVIL

Après cette scène où je me suis montré si éclatant de chasteté que peut-il advenir?

Où sont mes papiers et mon identité vieillie et la date de ma naissance imprécise? Et, d'ailleurs, suis-je encore celui de la dernière fois? Pourtant je croyais avoir repris suffisamment de forces. Et tout ce qu'on m'avait promis.

La tête s'écarte de la ligne bleue qui se déroule sur la longue route rugueuse. En dehors d'elle aucun salut possible et l'indifférence nous perd.

Voilà pour ta modestie, ton abstinence et ta faiblesse, sans cruauté. Mille dangers à craindre. Regarde, tourne ton œil vers cette nappe noire.

Sur le trottoir le gendarme souverain t'arrête d'un appel bref de sa question brutale.


## CORTÈGE

Quand les premiers furent passés et que l'on attendait encore.

Une voix s'éleva qui t'avertit.

Quand les derniers furent passes et que l'on n'entendit plus rien.

Qui t'a dit de rester là encore?

La dernière étoile résistait au matin et tu ne pouvais plus voir que la poussière. Sous tes pieds il n'y avait plus que de la poussière au loin et partout, et aussi tes souliers en étaient recouverts.

Et ce soir-là les questions t'accablèrent.

Tu les as vus passer et tu restes là. Le chant du coq t'avertit, le chant du coq ou la poussière t'avertissent que tes paupières sont lourdes, tes cils sont gris comme les buissons au bord de la route; il est temps d'aller dormir. Et tu les reverras peut-être tous en rêve.

## CIVIL

After this scene where I revealed myself so resplendently chaste what can happen?

Where are my papers and my identity grown old and the date of my imprecise birth? And besides, am I still the one from last time? Yet I thought I had gotten strong enough again. And everything I'd been promised.

The head moves away from the blue line unrolling down the long uneven road. Apart from it no salvation is possible and indifference destroys us.

So much for your modesty, your abstinence and your weakness, devoid of cruelty. A thousand dangers to fear. Look, gaze upon this black surface.

On the sidewalk the domineering gendarme stops you with a terse summons for a brutal questioning.


## PROCESSION

When the first ones had gone by and people were still waiting.

A voice was raised to warn you.

When the last ones had gone by and nothing more was heard.

Who told you to stay on there?

The last star was resisting the morning and you could no longer see anything but dust. Under your feet there was no longer anything but dust far off and everywhere: your shoes too were covered with it.

And that evening the questions assaulted you.

You saw them go by and you remain there. The cock's cry warns you, the cock's cry or the dust warn you that your eyelids are heavy, your lashes gray like the shrubs along the road; it is time to go and sleep. And perhaps you will see them all again, dreaming.

## TIMIDITÉ

Après un voyage trop long et des insomnies prolongées, seule la plus grande joie vient t'attendre.

Sans aucune certitude ni garantie avec tous les efforts, seulement permis et promis, tu n'es plus seul et prêt à marcher, n'importe où.

Le monde te confie sa force en échange de ta confiance. Tu ferais toutes les démarches si l'aplomb avait payé ton sort à ta naissance. Mais qui t'a mis cette hésitation poignante dans le ventre? Tes jambes n'auront jamais la force de ton énorme poids.

Sur le palier, plus haut que les marches qu'il n'a pas su compter, il hésite et, plus heureux qu'après une grande victoire, il redescend sans avoir seulement effleuré de sa main lâche le cordon auquel il aurait plutôt pendu son cou.


## APRÈS LE BAL

J'ai peut-être mis au vestiaire plus que mes vêtements. Je m'avance, allégé, avec trop d'assurance et quelqu'un dans la salle a remarqué mes pas. Les rayons sont pleins de danseuses.

Je tourne, je tourne sans rien voir dans les flots de rayons des lampes électriques et je marche sur tant de pieds et tant d'autres meurtrissent les miens.

Quel bal, quelle fête! J'ai trouvé toutes les femmes belles, tous mes désirs volent vers tous ces yeux. Tant qu'a duré l'orchestre j'ai tourné des talons sur un parquet ciré, plein d'émotion, et mes bras sont rompus d'avoir supporté tant de proies qu'il a fallu lâcher.

Mais l'orchestre s'est tu, les lampes éteintes ont laissé s'alourdir la fatigue. Au vestiaire, on m'a rendu un chaud manteau contre le gel, mais le reste? Il me manque pourtant quelque chose. Je suis seul et je ne puis lutter contre ce froid.

## TIMIDITY

After too long a trip and prolonged insomnia, only the greatest joy comes to await you.

With no certainty or guarantee from all the effort, only permitted and promised, you are no longer alone and ready to walk no matter where.

The world entrusts you with its strength in exchange for your confidence. You would make all the moves if aplomb had paid for your fate at birth. But who put this poignant hesitation in you? Your legs will never have the strength of your enormous weight.

On the landing, higher than the steps he never managed to count, he hesitates, and happier than after a great victory, he comes back down without having even so much as grazed with his limp hand the cord on which he would sooner have hung his neck.

## AFTER THE BALL

Perhaps I have left more than just my clothes in the cloakroom. I move forward, lightened, with too much self-assurance, and someone in the room has noticed my step. The light beams are filled with dancing women.

I am spinning, spinning about and seeing nothing in the beams flooding from the electric lights and walking on so many feet and so many others bruise mine.

What a dance, what a ball: I found the women lovely, and my desires rush forward toward those eyes. As long as the orchestra lasted, I spun my heels about on a waxed floor, full of emotion, and my arms are exhausted from propping up the preys I had then to desert.

But the orchestra fell silent, the extinguished lamps let my fatigue grow heavy. In the cloakroom they gave me back a warm coat against the frost, but the rest? Something still is missing. Alone, I cannot struggle against this cold.

## VOYAGES TROP GRANDS

C'était peut-être la première fois qu'il voyait quelque chose de clair. Il se sentait accroché au dernier wagon du train de luxe pour quelque destination magnifique et regardait distraitement le paysage qui allait, à rebours, bien plus vite que lui. Avec la somme de tous les détails perdus on aurait fait un nouveau monde; mais lui n'avait besoin de rien. De son rôle, qu'il jouait avec le plus grand sérieux, il lui manquait la signification.

Les plus grandes gares n'avaient pas assez de bruit pour l'émouvoir; au coin de toutes les collines il comprenait mieux l'isolement des maisons blanches. Quand on longeait la mer il ne voyait que les voiles des barques qui en précisaient l'étendue.

Tout est inerte et trop grand pour ses yeux et son cœur. Sa tête doit rester vide et rien ne pourrait la remplir.

Quand il revenait enfin là d'où il était parti, sa tâche bien remplie, sa journée faite il ne pensait qu'au petit coin de terre où sa vie contenait, où il aurait la place juste pour mourir.


## CHACUN SA PART

Il a chassé la lune, il a laissé la nuit. Une à une les étoiles sont tombées dans un filet d'eau vive.

Derrière les trembles un étrange pêcheur guette avec impatience d'un œil ouvert, le seul, caché sous son large chapeau; et la ligne frémit.

Rien ne se prend, mais il emplit sa gibecière de pièces d'or dont l'éclat s'est éteint dans le panier fermé.

Mais un autre attendait plus loin du bord. Plus modeste il pêchait dans la flaque de boue qu'avait laissée la pluie. Cette eau, venue du ciel, était pleine d'étoiles.

## TRIPS IN EXCESS

It was perhaps the first time he had seen anything clear. He felt hooked to the last car of the first-class train headed for some magnificent destination and looked absentmindedly at the landscape, which was going backwards much faster than he was. A new world could have been created with all the lost details; but he needed nothing. He saw no meaning in his role, which he was playing with the greatest possible seriousness.

The biggest stations did not have enough noise to move him; in the corner of all the hills he better understood the isolation of the white houses. When they went alongside the sea, he saw only the sails of the boats, revealing its reach.

Everything is inert and too large for his eyes and his heart. His head had to remain empty and nothing could ever fill it.

When he came back at last to the place where he had started, his task completed, his day finished, he thought only of the little corner of earth where his life fit in, where he would have just enough room to die.

## TO EACH HIS SHARE

He chased the moon and left the night. One by one the stars fell into a net of living water.

Behind the quaking aspens, a strange fisherman waits impatiently, with one eye open, the only one, hidden under his wide hat; and the line quivers.

Nothing gets caught, but he fills his game-bag with gold pieces whose gleam is extinguished in the closed basket.

But another is waiting further from the shore. More modestly, he was fishing in the mud puddle left by the rain. This water, having come from the sky, was filled with stars.

## BRUITS DE NUIT

Au moment où les chevaux passaient, la suspension trembla. Le plafond menaçait de se pencher à droite, contre nos têtes; mais les fenêtres restaient d'aplomb avec le ciel, et l'on voyait le paysage nocturne.

Il n'y avait plus de hiboux dans les ruines, plus de rayon de lune parmi les arbres, mais une cheminée d'usine et — autour — des maisons dont les toits avaient l'air de grandir.

Et les chevaux — dont on entendait les pas précipités — transportaient dans la nuit complice des fourgons de mort en métal.

## FRONTS DE BATAILLE

Sur le rempart où tremblent des ruines on entend un écho de tambours. On les avait crevés. Ceux d'hier se répondent encore.

La nuit finie, le bruit dissipe les rêves et les fronts découverts où saigne une blessure.

Au milieu des fumées les hommes sont perdus et déjà le soleil transperce l'horizon.

Qui sonna la victoire? La charge bat pour ceux qui sont tombés!

Une trompette rallie des lambeaux d'escadrons et la fumée soutient les chevaux dont les pieds ne touchent plus le sol.

Mais celui qui les aurait peints n'était plus là.

## NIGHT SOUNDS

At the moment when the horses were passing by the hanging lamp started to quiver. The ceiling threatened to lean to the right, against our heads; but the windows remained upright with the sky, and the nocturnal landscape was visible.

No longer were there owls among the ruins, nor moon beams among the trees, but a factory chimney and — around it — houses whose roofs seemed to grow.

And the horses — whose hurried steps were heard — transported into the accomplice night the metal wagons of death.


## BATTLEFRONTS

On the rampart where ruins are trembling an echo of drums is heard. They had been shattered. Those of yesterday still respond to each other now.

Once night is finished, the noise dissipates the dreams and the bared foreheads where a wound is bleeding.

Amid the smoke, men are lost and already the sun pierces through the horizon.

Who rang the sounds of victory: The volley laments those fallen.

A trumpet rallies the tatters of squadrons and the smoke holds up the horses whose hoofs no longer touch the ground.

But he who would have painted them was no longer there.

## BATAILLE

Dans la poitrine, l'amour d'un drapeau décoloré par les pluies. Dans ma tête, les tambours battent. Mais d'où vient l'ennemi?

Si ta foi est morte que répondre à leur commandement?

Un ami meurt d'enthousiasme derrière ses canons et sa fatigue est plus forte que tout.

Et, dans les champs bordés de routes, au coin des bois qui ont une autre forme parce qu'il y a des hommes cachés, il se promène, macabre comme la mort, malgré son ventre.

Les ruines balancent leurs cadavres et des têtes sans képis.

Ce tableau, soldat, quand le finiras-tu? Ai-je rêvé que j'y étais encore? Je faisais, en tout cas, un drôle de métier.

Quand le soleil, que j'avais pris pour un éclair, darda son rayon sur mon oreille sourde, je me désaltérais, sous les saules vert et blanc, dans un ruisseau d'eau rose.

J'avais si soif!


## FACE À FACE

Il s'avance et la raideur de son pas timide trahit son assurance. Les regards ne quittent pas ses pieds. Tout ce qui luit dans ces yeux, d'où jaillissent de mauvaises pensées, éclaire sa marche hésitante. Il va tomber.

Au fond de la salle une image connue se dresse. Sa main tendue va vers la sienne. Il ne voit plus rien que ça; mais il se heurte, tout à coup, contre lui-même.


## SALTIMBANQUES

Au milieù de cet attroupement il y a avec un enfant qui danse un homme qui soulève des poids. Ses bras tatoués de bleu prennent le ciel à témoin de leur force inutile.

L'enfant danse, léger, dans un maillot trop grand; plus léger que les boules où il se tient en équilibre. Et quand il tend son escarcelle, personne ne donne. Personne ne donne de peur de la remplir d'un poids trop lourd. Il est si maigre.

BATTLE

In the breast the love of a flag discolored by the rains. In my head drums are beating. But where is the enemy coming from?

If your faith is dead, how will you answer their command?

A friend dies from enthusiasm behind his cannons and his fatigue is stronger than all else.

And in the fields edged by the roads, in the corner of the woods differently-shaped because of the men hidden there, he walks, macabre as death, in spite of his stomach.

The ruins dangle their cadavers and hatless heads.

This painting, soldier, when will you finish it? Did I dream I was still there? In any case I was doing a funny job.

When the sun, which I'd taken for a lightning flash, darted its beam on my deaf ear, I quenched my thirst, under the green and white willows, in a stream of pink water.

I was so thirsty!


FACE TO FACE

He is moving forward and the stiffness of his timid step belies his assurance. Attention is focused on his feet. Everything shining in these eyes, which radiate evil thoughts, makes clear the hesitation of his gait. He is about to fall.

In the back of the room a well-known figure stands up. Its hand, held out, reaches for his. He sees only that and nothing else; but he collides, suddenly, with himself.


ACROBATS

In the middle of the crowd there is, with a dancing child, a man lifting weights. His arms tattooed in blue call on the sky to bear witness to their useless strength.

Lightly, the child dances, in tights which are too big for him; lighter than the balls he balances on. And when he holds out his purse, no one gives anything. No one gives for fear of making it too heavy. He is so thin.

## CRÉPUSCULE

Le soir tombant dilatait les yeux du chat.

Nous étions tous les deux assis sur la fenêtre et nous regardions, nous écoutions tout ce qui n'était pas autre part qu'en nous-mêmes.

Derrière la ligne qui fermait la rue, la ligne d'en haut, les arbres découpaient de la dentelle sur le ciel.

Et la ville, où est-elle la ville qui se noie au fond dans l'eau qui forme les nuages?

## L'ENVERS À L'ENDROIT

Il grimpe sans jamais s'arrêter, sans jamais se retourner et personne que lui ne sait où il va.

Le poids qu'il traîne est lourd mais ses jambes sont libres et il n'a pas d'oreilles.

A chaque porte il a crié son nom, personne n'a ouvert.

Mais quand il a su qu'on attendait quelqu'un et qui, il a su transformer son visage. Alors il est entré à la place de celui qu'on attendait et qui ne venait pas.

## LES PENSÉES BASSES

*Les quatre pieds de la table sont immobiles; les autres aussi. Et vos têtes! Vos têtes qui se penchent dans vos mains pour ne pas qu'on les voie rougir?*

## TWILIGHT

The fall of evening dilated the cat's eyes.

We were both seated by the window and looking, listening to everything which was nowhere but in ourselves.

Behind the line closing the street, and above it, the trees traced patterns of lace cut-outs upon the sky.

And the town, where is the town submerged in the depths of the water forming the clouds?

## THE WRONG SIDE ON THE RIGHT SIDE

He climbs, never stopping, never turning around, and no one but himself knows where he is going.

The weight he drags along is heavy, but his legs are free and he has no ears.

At each door he shouted his name; no one opened.

But when he found out they were awaiting someone and whom, he was able, to alter his face. Then he entered in the place of the one awaited, who never came.

## LOW THOUGHTS

*The four feet of the table are immobile; the others too. And your faces! Your faces cupped in your hands so no one will see them blushing?*

Selection from

# *Le Cadran Quadrillé*
# *(The Gridded Dial)*

1915

Translated by Mary Ann Caws

## QUEL TOURBILLON

En haut du chemin sur l'horizon où le vent tombe déjà, il part sans se retourner ni dire adieu. Derrière les arbres, le village s'endort et les vitres s'allument. Plus loin ce sont des illuminations monstres et des agglomérations dont l'ampleur alourdit son esprit étonné. Il se jette au monde dans des bras inconnus et tourne au bruit nouveau qui hante ses oreilles. On annonce l'exil parmi les orages et les pluies de soleil nocturne de la ville. Des cérémonies traînent pendant des heures devant le jardin en fleurs et la mairie. Mais il faut toujours tenir compte du cadre. Enfin, si quelquefois le temps a réussi, on peut revenir par un chemin tout neuf et un autre paysage. Et c'est un air plus chaud qui va dans la poitrine. D'autres visages aperçus entre les éclaircies. Une autre lumière qui brûle les yeux fait fondre les nuages. Pendant que le calme et le silence renaissent et que tout reprend de justes proportions dans la campagne.

## TOUJOURS L'AUTRE

Il y eut, tout le temps que dura l'orage,
quelqu'un qui parla sous le couvert.
    Autour de la lumière que
      traçait son doigt sur la nappe
    on aurait pu voir de grosses lettres noires
        en regardant bien.
Bientôt ce fut un autre ton
    et la couleur du mur changea
La voix semblait venir de derrière
    On ne savait pas si c'était le mur
      ou le paravent.
    Les lettres disparurent
ou plutôt elles s'étaient réunies et
formaient un nom étranger
      qu'on ne déchiffrait pas

## WHAT A WHIRLWIND

At the rise of the path on the horizon where the wind is already falling, he departs without a backward glance or a farewell. Behind the trees, the village is drifting to sleep and its windows are lighting up. Further on, there are gigantic illuminations and agglomerations whose size weighs heavily on his astonished mind. He hurls himself into the world between unknown arms and turns at the unaccustomed noise haunting his ears. Exile is announced among the storms, and the rains of nightly sun on the town. Ceremonies drag on for hours in front of the flowering garden and the town hall. But the frame must always be considered. Finally, if time has succeeded now and again, an entirely new path of return can be taken in, another landscape. And a warmer air streams into the lungs. Other faces perceived between the clearings. Another light burning the eyes melts the clouds. While calm and silence are reborn and everything takes on its right proportions in the countryside.

## ALWAYS THE OTHER

There was, as long as the storm lasted,
someone speaking under cover
    Around the light that
      his finger was tracing on the cloth
      large black letters were to be seen
         if you looked closely
Soon it was another tone
    and the color of the wall changed
The voice seemed to come from behind
    was it the wall
       or the screen
    The letters disappeared
or rather merged to
form an unfamiliar name
      impossible to read

Selection from

# Quelques poèmes (Some Poems)

1916

Translated by Mary Ann Caws

Le masque honteux cachait ses dents. Un autre œil voyait qu'elles étaient fausses. Où cela se passe-t-il? Et quand? Il est seul, il pleure, malgré l'orguei qui le soutient, et il devient laid. Parce qu'il a plu sur les souliers, disait l'autre, de la salive sur mes souliers, je suis devenu pâle et méchant. Et il embrassa le masque qui le mordit en ricanant.

Le profil, le même profil que la grande chanteuse! Elle voulait l'avoir, elle l'eut et aussi son immense bouche sans sa voix. Mais ce qu'elle enviait le plus c'était sa robe et jamais elle ne put l'avoir.

Si vous entendez derrière vous faire Psst et qu'en même temps passe un taxi ne vous retournez pas ... c'est pour le taxi.

Les cheveux coupés, la tête tranchêe, le sabre restait encore entre ses dents. Le bourreau amateur pleurait et sa figure êtait un masque. On l'avait importé de Chine et il ne savait plus être cruel.

Je passé en m'engouff-rant, je m'engouffre en passant. Quel gouf-fre! La tête qui tour-nait autour de moi a disparus. — Les Oiseaux chantaient derrière la fenêtre; ils chantaient faux et n'étaient pas en plumes véritables.

# SQUARES

The shameful mask hid his teeth.
Another eye saw they were false. Where
is it happening? And when? He is alone,
weeping, despite the pride bearing him
up, and he becomes ugly. Because it has
rained on the shoes, the other one said,
saliva on my shoes, I have become pale
and wicked. And he kissed the mask
which bit him as it sneered.

The profile, the same profile
as the great singer! She
wanted to have it, she had it
and also her mammoth mouth
without her voice. But what
she most envied was the
singer's dress and never could
she have it.

If you hear someone behind
you go Psst and a taxi is pass-
ing at the same time don't
turn around ... it's for the
taxi.

The hair cut, the head sev-
ered, the saber still remained
between his teeth. The am-
ateur executioner was weep-
ing and his face was a mask.
He had been imported from
China and no longer knew
how to be cruel.

I pass by being swallowed
up, am swallowed up in a
passing by. What an abyss!
The head turning about me
has disappeared. The birds
were singing behind the win-
dow; they were singing off-
key and were not dressed in
real feathers.

Le rhum est excellent
la pipe est amère et les
étoiles qui tombent de
vos cheveux s'envolent
dans la cheminée.

De la reliure de tes
lèvres de la reliure de
tes volets de la reliure
de nos mains. O peut-
etre plus facile! Sur le
balcon de bois elle
montait la garde en
chemise éclatante.

Après les premiers pas
sur les pointes il avait
pris son vol. Les pre-
miers nuages l'arrêtent.
Ce sont des glaces.
Et là, où il retrouvait
notre monde sans la
chair, il se crut au ciel.

The rum is excellent
The pipe is bitter and
the stars falling from
your hair fly off in
the fireplace.

From the binding of your lips from the binding of your shutters from the binding of our hands. Or perhaps easier. On the wooden balcony she kept watch in a dazzling nightgown.

After the first steps on his toes he had taken flight. The first clouds stop him. They are mirrors. And here again, where he discovered our world without flesh, he believed himself in heaven.

Selection from

# *La Lucarne ovale*
# *(The Oval Attic Window)*
## 1916

Translated by Mary Ann Caws

## TOUJOURS GÊNÉ

Qui m'a révélé l'endroit précis. Le ciel où les deux murs se joignent. L'angle où l'on est à l'abri?

Par-dessus, le vent emporte la terre qui se déplace. Quelques nids sont tombés et l'on entend des cris qui viennent des fenêtres. C'est là qu'on attend. C'est de là qu'on regarde et qu'on nous surprend. L'affreuse tête qui se balance sur le toit en ricanant! Ni le mur ni les arbres ne sont assez grands.

Et déjà vous commencez à rougir plus que moi-même. Allons-nous-en.

## ENCORE MARCHER

S'il se soulève quand je passerai près de lui; s'il pleure quand viendra la nuit, s'il ne crie pas? J'aurai cru le voir et ce sera fini.

Plusieurs heures de chemin dans un sentier où l'herbe ne vit plus. J'ai marché bien longtemps et je me suis perdu. Je n'osais plus revenir sur mes pas ni appeler. Et je sentais derrière moi ses yeux qui me cherchaient.

Une faible lumière au loin s'allume entre les arbres. Une fenêtre où je ne pourrai pas frapper. Le feu où l'on refuse de me laisser réchauffer. Et je n'ai même pas le droit de m'arrêter. Un mur en face de moi s'est mis à reculer.

Les cloches sonnent au clocher d'un village lointain et je ne sais que faire de mes mains. Avancer malgré le vent et la nuit qui monte lentement. Je n'ai pas de manteau. Dans l'ombre j'entendais le pas de leurs chevaux.

Où vas-tu me mener? L'auberge où l'on descend est trop loin pour y aller. Les gens s'en vont je ne sais où; je les suivrai. Quand une main d'enfant m'a fait signe de rester. Et seul je suis perdu là devant vous, devant vous tous et je ne peux plus m'en aller.

## ALWAYS BOTHERED

Who revealed to me the precise place. The sky where the two walls join. The angle where you are sheltered?

Above, the wind carries off the earth which shifts position. A few nests have fallen and you hear cries coming from the windows. The waiting place, where they look out, and catch us off guard. The awful head as it sways sneering on the roof. Neither the wall nor the trees are tall enough.

And you are already beginning to blush more than I am. Let's go away.


## TO KEEP ON WALKING

If he raises himself when I pass near him; if he weeps when the night comes, if he does not cry out? I shall have thought I saw him and it will all be over.

Many hours of walking in a path where grass grows no longer. I walked quite a while and was lost. I dared not take the same path back or call out. And behind me I felt his eyes looking for me.

A faint glow in the distance lights up between the trees. A window I cannot knock on. The fire where they will not let me warm myself. And I have not even the right to stop. Across from me a wall has started to pull back.

In the steeple tower of a distant village the bells are ringing, and what should I do with my hands? To go forward in spite of the wind and the night slowly coming on. I have no coat. In the shadow, I heard their horses' hoofs.

Where will you lead me? The inn where people stay is too far to reach. The people are going off who knows where; I shall follow them. When a child's hand signaled me to stay. And alone I am lost, there in front of you, in front of all of you, and I cannot go away.

## AUTRE FACE

Les yeux noirs! Mais ce sont des lorgnons! Une ombre glisse sur les joues. Deux larmes qui coulent sur les joues. Est-ce pour moi ou bien à cause du soleil? Personne n'ose demander qui ils regardent et chacun prend ce regard pour soi. Je crains d'être trop petit et trop loin. Moi, je suis certainement trop loin et celui qui est devant moi se: rapproche. Pour me rassurer je me dis que les yeux ne peuvent pas tout voir et qu'il ne reste au cœur rien que ce qu'il peut contenir.

## SON SEUL PASSAGE

Sur le bord du chemin où il s'est laissé tomber, les bras pendants, ses mains traînent dans le ruisseau où l'eau ne coule pas. La forêt s'ouvre sur sa tête et d'en haut le passant regarde le chemin. Il attend; aucun bruit ne court ailleurs que dans les branches où passe le vent. Le silence a désolé son cœur solitaire et fermé.

Un chien qui mord, une roue qui crie sur le gravier un moment secoueraient sa torpeur. Mais pour lui le monde est une route interminable où l'on se perd. Il a laissé dans les buissons ses souvenirs et les années passées sans rien comprendre.

La forêt qui l'arrête est un abri où il fuit le soleil et il regarde, sans la voir, monter la route vers les arbres. Plus loin le village s'endort étendu dans les champs que la nuit assombrit, mais pas une fenêtre en l'éclairant ne lui sourit.

## ANOTHER FACE

Those dark eyes! But they are opera glasses! A shadow slides over the cheeks. Two tears are running down the cheeks. Because of me or the sun? No one dares to ask, who they are looking at and each takes this look for himself. I'm afraid I'm too little and too far off. I'm certainly too far off and the one before me comes nearer. For reassurance, I tell myself that eyes cannot see everything and that there remains in the heart nothing but what it can hold.


## HIS ONLY PASSAGE

At pathside where he let himself fall, his arms dragging, his hands are trailing in the stream where the water does not run. The forest opens over his head and from above, the passerby contemplates the path. He is waiting; no sound but in the branches where the wind is moving. The silence has made desolation in his closed and solitary heart.

A dog biting, a wheel screeching on the gravel for an instant would shake off his torpor…But for him the world is an interminable road where one is lost. In the bushes he has left his memories and the years which have passed by with no understanding.

The forest which stops him is a shelter for him to flee the sun, and he looks at the road climbing towards the trees, not seeing it. Further on, the village dozes stretched out in the fields made somber by the night, but not a window lighting up for him.

Un. cortège de gens plus ou moins honorables. Quelques-uns sourient dans le vide avec sérénité. Ils sont nus. Une auréole à la tête des premiers qui ont su prendre la place. Les plus petits en queue.

On passe entre les arbres qui s'inclinent. Les esprits qui se sont réfugiés derrière les étoiles regardent. La curiosité vient de partout. La route s'illumine.

Dans le silence digne, si quelqu'un chante c'est une douce voix qui monte et personne ne rit. La chanson est connue de tous.

On passe devant la maison d'un poète qui n'est pas là. La pluie qui tombait sur son piano, à travers le toit, l'a chassé. Bientôt, c'est un boulevard bordé de cafés où la foule s'ennuie. Tout le monde se lève. Le cortège a grossi.

Enfin par l'avenue qui monte la file des gens s'éloigne, les derniers paraissent les plus grands. Les premiers ont déjà disparu.

Derrière un monument d'une époque oubliée le soleil se lève en rayons séparés et l'ombre des passants lentement s'efface. Les rideaux sont tirés.

## THE RIDICULOUS BODIES OF THE SPIRITS

A procession of more or less honorable people. Some of them smile into emptiness serenely. They are naked. A halo around the head of the first ones who managed to take their places. The littlest ones trailing behind.

They pass between the bending trees. The spirits who have taken refuge behind the stars are looking. Curiosity on all sides. The road lights up.

In the dignified silence, a sweet voice sings and no one laughs. Everyone knows the song.

They are passing by the house of a poet not at home. The rain falling on his piano through the roof sent him away.

Soon there is a boulevard lined with cafés where the crowds are bored. Everyone rises. The procession has grown.

Finally along the rising avenue, the line of people goes off, the last ones seeming tallest. The first ones have already disappeared.

Behind a monument to a forgotten time the sun is rising with separate beams and the shadows of the passersby fade slowly. The curtains are drawn.

# Les Ardoises du toit
# (Roof Slates)
## 1918

### Translated by Patricia Terry

Sur chaque ardoise
               qui glissait du toit
           on
          avait écrit
              un poème


La gouttière est bordée de diamants
                  les oiseaux les boivent


## FAÇADE

Par la fenêtre
         La nouvelle
Entre
         Vous n'êtes pas pressé
 Et la voix douce qui t'appelle
Indique où il faut regarder
        Rappelle-toi
            Le jour se lève
      Les signes que faisait ta main
Derrière un rideau
           Le matin
A fait une grimace brève
Le soleil crève sa prunelle
        Nous sommes deux sur le chemin

On every slate
        sliding from the roof
            someone
        had written
            a poem


The gutter is rimmed with diamonds
                        the birds drink them




FAÇADE

Through the window
                    Something new
Comes in
            There is plenty of time
And the gentle voice calling you
Lets you know where to look
                Remember
                            It's getting light
        The gestures of your hand
Behind a curtain
                    Morning
Suddenly made a face
The sun bursts the apple of its eye
            There are two of us on the road

## RÉCLAME

Hangar monté
                    la porte ouverte
Le ciel
            En haut deux mains se sont offertes
Les yeux levés
                    Une voix monte
Les toits se sont mis à trembler
Le vent lance des feuilles mortes
Et les nuages retardés
Marchent vers l'autre bout du monde
Qui se serait mis à siffler
Dans le calme d'un soir d'été
Le chant
            L'oiseau
                    Les étoiles
Et la lune pour t'écouter


## MATIN

La fontaine coule sur la place du port d'été
Le soleil déridé brille au travers de l'eau
Les voix qui murmuraient sont bien plus lointaines
Il en reste encore quelques frais lambeaux
J'écoute le bruit
                    Mais elles où sont-elles
Que sont devenus leurs paniers fleuris
Les murs limitaient la profondeur de la foule
Et le vent dispersa les têtes qui parlaient
Les voix sont restées à peu près pareilles
Les mots sont posés à mes deux oreilles
Et le moindre cri les fait s'envoler

HAWKING

Raised hangar
                    the door open
The sky
            Up there two hands extended
Lifted eyes
                A voice rises
The roofs have begun to tremble
The wind launches dead leaves
And the clouds delayed
Set out for the other end of the world
Which perhaps had begun to whistle
In the calm of a summer evening
The song
            The bird
                        The stars
And the moon to listen to you


MORNING

The fountain flows in the square of the summer harbor
Smooth-browed the sun is gleaming through the water
Those murmuring voices are very much farther away
Just a few cool fragments remain
For me to hear
                But they where are they
What has become of their baskets full of flowers
The walls determined the thickness of the crowd
And the wind dispersed the heads in conversation
The voices are really very much the same
The words have come to rest on my two ears
And the slightest outcry makes them fly away

## FEU

Enfin le vent plus libre passe
La pointe fléchit sur sa trace
Une vague s'efface plus loin
Sur le champ le plan monte
                    Le ciel s'incline lentement
Un lambeau de nuage flotte
Plus sombre par-dessus le mur
                    L'espace s'agrandit
Et là devant
          Quelqu'un qui n'a rien dit
          Deux yeux
          Une double lumière
Qui vient de franchir la barrièr
          En s'abattant


## GRAND'ROUTE

Le feu est presque éteint
          Et devant quelqu'un pleure
Où passe cette main
      Dont la chaleur demeure

Il fait nuit
      Les vitres se fondent

Si la maison disparaissait
      Avec nous derrière les arbres
Quelqu'un encore resterait
Une voix douce chanterait
                    Et l'ombre du temps s'en irait
Le soir
      Faire le tour du monde


84

FIRE

At last the freer wind passes
The tip bends down in its path
A more distant wave surrenders
Thereupon the field's level rises
                          The sky bows slowly down
A fragment of cloud floats
Darker above the wall
                    Space expands
And there in front
                Someone who hasn't said anything
                Two eyes
                A double light
    Just forced its way through the barrier
                By knocking itself out


HIGHWAY

The fire has almost gone out
            And close to it someone in tears
Where has that hand moved on
        Whose warmth is still here

It is dark
        The windows melt

If the house were to disappear
        With us behind the trees
Someone would still remain
A gentle voice would be singing
                          And the shadow of time would go away
In the evening
            To travel the world

## LE SOIR

Jour à jour ta vie est un immeuble qui s'élève
Des fenêtres fermées des fenêtres ouvertes
    Et la porte noire au milieu
Ce qui brille dans ta figure
                        Les yeux
        Tristes les souvenirs glissent sur
      ta poitrine
Devant part vers en haut l'espoir
La douceur du repos qui revient chaque soir
Tu es assis devant la porte
    Tête inclinée
                Dans l'ombre qui s'étend
Le calme qui descend
Une prière monte
On ne voit pas les genoux de celui qui prie

IN THE EVENING

Day by day your life is a building going up
There are closed windows open windows
    And the black door
What illuminates your face
                        Your eyes
    Sad the memories gliding over
    your breast
In front there is hope ascending
The sweetness of rest returning in the evening
You sit in front of the door
    With your head bowed
                     In the widening shadow
The calm drifting down
A prayer rises
The knees of someone praying can't be seen

## AUBERGE

Un œil se ferme

      Au fond plaquée contre le mur
      la pensée qui ne sort pas

      Des idées s'en vont pas à pas

   On pourrait mourir
Ce que je tiens entre mes bras pourrait partir
    Un rêve
L'aube à peine née qui s'achève
    Un cliquetis
Les volets en s'ouvrant l'ont abolie

     Si rien n'allait venir

Il y a un champ où l'on pourrait encore courir
            Des étoiles à n'en plus finir
     Et ton ombre au bout de l'avenue
      Elle s'efface

On n'a rien vu
De tout ce qui passait on n'a rien retenu
 Autant de paroles qui montent
Des contes qu'on n'a jamais lus
          Rien
Les jours qui se pressent à la sortie
    Enfin la cavalcade s'est évanouie

En bas entre les tables où l'on jouait aux cartes

INN

An eye closes

     Deep inside and flat against the wall
     the thought which doesn't go out

     Ideas step by step go their way

   Death could happen
What I hold in my arms could slip away
    A dream
Dawn at its birth dies out
     In a clatter
Of opening shutters annulled

     If nothing were going to come

There's a field where we could still run
                 Unlimited stars
       And your shadow where the avenue comes to an end
            Vanishing

We have seen nothing
Of all that was passing we held on to nothing
So many words rising
Stories we never read
            Nothing
The days in a rush for the exit
       At last the cavalcade has faded out

Down there between the tables where we played cards

# CADRAN

Sur la lune
               s'inscrit
                         Un mot
La lettre la plus grande en haut
Elle est humide comme un œil
La moitié se ferme
               Et le ciel
                            Se couvre
       Un lourd rideau qu'on ouvre
Sans bruit
                    Une lumière luit
Rapide
C'est une autre lueur à présent
          qui me guide

DIAL

On the moon
        is inscribed
            A word
With its tallest letter on top
Moist as an eye
Half of it closes
     And the sky
            Clouds over
  A heavy curtain is opened
Soundlessly
         A quick light
Gleams
It's another glow just now
  that guides me

## ABAT-JOUR

Autour de la table
            Au bord de l'ombre
 Aucun d'eux ne remue beaucoup
Et quelqu'un parle tout à coup
Il fait froid dehors
        Mais là c'est le calme
Et la lumière les unit
                Le feu pétille
Une étincelle
            Les mains se sont posées
            Plus bleues sur le tapis
Derrière le rayon une tété qui lit
            Un souffle qui s'échappe à peine
Tout s'endort
 Le silence traîne
            Mais il faut encore rester
La vitre reproduit le tableau
            La famille
De loin toutes les lèvres ont l'air d'être ferventes et
    de prier

## LIGHTSHADE

Around the table
           On the shadow's edge
Each one of them quite motionless
And someone abruptly speaks
It's cold outside
   But here it's peaceful
And the light holds them together
              The fire crackles
A spark
        The hands have come to rest
        Bluer on top of the tablecloth
Behind the beam of light a head reads
        Nearly holding its breath
Everything's falling asleep
The silence drags on
        But still it is not time to go
The windowpane mirrors the scene
        The family
From a distance the lips all seem to be fervent and
   praying

## TARD DANS LA NUIT …

La couleur que décompose la nuit
La table où ils se sont assis
Le verre en cheminée
              La lampe est un cœur qui se vide
C'est une autre année
          Une nouvelle ride
Y aviez-vous déjà pensé
                  La fenêtre déverse un carré bleu
La porte est plus intime
        Une séparation
              Le remords et le crime
Adieu je tombe
Dans l'angle doux des bras qui me reçoivent
Du coin de l'œil je vois tous ceux qui boivent
              Je n'ose pas bouger
 Ils sont assis
                      La table est ronde
Et ma mémoire aussi
Je me souviens de tout le monde
Même de ceux qui sont partis


## SUR LE TALUS

Le soir couchant ferme une porte
Nous sommes au bord du chemin
Dans l'ombre
        près du ruisseau où tout se tient

Si c'est encore une lumière
                  La ligne part à l'infini

L'eau monte comme une poussière

              Le silence ferme la nuit

LATE AT NIGHT ...

The color night disintegrates
They are sitting around the table
The chimney glass
          The lamp giving out like a heart
It's another year
    One more wrinkle
Had you thought of that before
          The window pours out a square of blue
More personal is the door
    A separation
              Remorse and crime
Farewell I'm falling
Into the gentle angle of open arms
I see the drinkers from the corner of my eye
          To move could be dangerous
They sit there
                The table is round
My memory is too
I remember everyone
Even those who have gone


ON THE BANK

Evening as it sets closes a door
We are on the edge of the road
In the shadow
    close to the brook where everything waits

If that's one more line of light
          It's heading for infinity

The water rises like a kind of dust

          Silence closes the night

## ROUTE

Sur le seuil personne
      Ou ton ombre
Un souvenir qui resterait
La route passe
    Et les arbres parlent plus près
Qu'y a-t-il derrière
        Un mur
            des voix
Les nuages qui s'élevèrent
Au moment où je passais là
Et tout le long une barrière
      Où sont ceux qui n'entreront pas


## SUR LE SEUIL

Dans le coin où elle s'est blottie
        Tristesse ou vide
Le vent tourne
        On entend un cri
Personne n'a voulu se plaindre
Mais la lampe vient de s'éteindre
     Et passe sans faire de bruit
Une main tiède
     Sur tes paupières
     Où pèse la journée finie
Tout se dresse
     Et dans le monde qui se presse
Les objets mêlés à la nuit
      La forme que j'avais choisie
Si la lumière
     Revivait conme on se réveille
Il resterait dans mon oreille
La voix joyeuse qui la veille
En rentrant m'avait poursuivi

## ROAD

On the threshold no one
     Or your shadow
A lingering memory
The road passes by
     And the trees come closer as they talk
What is there behind
       A wall
          voices
The clouds that lifted
Just as I was passing by
And all along a barrier
       Where are those who shall not enter


## ON THE THRESHOLD

Where she is huddled into a corner
       Emptiness or pain
The wind circles
       A cry is heard
No one went to complain
But the lamp has just gone out
     And silently passes
A hand warm
     On your eyelids
     Weighed down by the end of the day
Everything stiffens upright
      And in the rush of the crowd
Where objects merge into night
       The form that I had in mind
If light
     Came to life again as we do out of sleep
There would remain in my ear
The joyful voice that the day before
Tried to follow me all the way home

## ABÎME

Je m'attendais à tout ce qui peut arriver
La tête en bas
        Les pieds touchant la tête
Et tout ce qui dans l'angle remuait
Contre le mur
        En face et par côté
La glace qui s'éteint s'était mise à trembler
Il y avait une lumière
            Autrefois
Et la figure que je vois
         Minuit
      Serait-ce l'heure
Sous le toit la gouttière pleure
Et le train au loin qui criait
La chambre s'étendait bien plus loin que les murs

Alors on aurait pu m'atteindre
        Ou même j'aurais pu tomber

Le monde pour dormir se renversait

ABYSS

I was expecting anything that can happen
Upside down
      Feet touching my head
And whatever stirred in the corner
Against the wall
      Opposite and to one side
As it went out the mirror began to tremble
There was a light
        Once
And the face I can see
      Midnight
     Would this be the time
Under the roof the rainspout weeps
And the train crying out in the distance
The bedroom extended far beyond the walls

They could have gotten to me then
     I could even have fallen

The world ready for sleep was turning over

## DÉPART

L'horizon s'incline
Les jours sont plus longs
Voyage
Un cœur saute dans une cage
Un oiseau chante
Il va mourir
Une autre porte va s'ouvrir
Aù fond du couloir
Où s'allume
Une étoile
Une femme brune
La lanterne du train qui part


## UNE ÉCLAIRCIE

Il fait plus noir
Les yeux se ferment
La prairie se dressait plus claire
Dans l'air il y avait un mouchoir
Et tu faisais des signes
Ta main sortait sous la manche du soir
Je voulais franchir la barrière
Quelqùe chose me retenait
Le cri venait de .loin
Par derrière la nuit
Et tout ce qui s'avance
Et tout ce que je fuis
Encore
Je me rappelle
La rue que le matin inondait de soleil

## DEPARTURE

The horizon leans down
        The days are longer
        Travelling
    A heart leaps up in its cage
        A bird sings
        It is going to die
There will be another door open
      At the end of the corridor
        Now glows
        A star
A woman with dark hair
    The lantern of the departing train


## A BREAK IN THE CLOUDS

It's getting darker
        Eyes close
The plain was rising up brighter
    There was a handkerchief in the air
And you were beckoning
        Your hand emerging from an evening sleeve
I wanted to cross the barrier
        Something was holding me back
The cry was coming from far away
        From the other side of the night
And all that comes forward
        And all that I flee
Still
        I remember
The street that morning filled to the brim with sunlight

## LENDEMAIN

Une ombre était passée ce soir sur le fronton
Sur la bande du ciel
       Et sur la plaine ouverte
       Où tombait un rayon
Elle restait immobile
       Aurait-on pu de loin
    Entendre seulement le cri d'une sirène
Et tout ce qui marchait
Sur la terre et dans l'air
Plus vite
       Elle s'envolait
       Il ne restait plus bas
       Que les gens inhabiles
       Ceux qui les retenaient
Et moi
       Regardant la lumière tremblante
La rue qui se laissait aller
Tout seul devant ma vie passée
Et par où commencer le jour qui se présente

## NEXT DAY

This evening a shadow passed over the pediment
Over the strip of sky
       And the open plain
       Where a ray of light was falling
To stand immobile
       Could one only have heard
   In the distance a siren's cry
And all that was moving
On the earth and in the air
More quickly
       It flew away
       Nothing was left lower down
       But the incapable people
       Those who were holding them back
And myself
       To watch the light tremble
The street let itself go
All alone to face the life that I've lived
And where to begin with the day that is coming to meet me

# RONDE NOCTURNE

Le timbre vient de loin
Les mondes se rapprochent
Sur les bords du clocher des étoiles s'accrochent
Dans le coin des cheminées fument
Ce sont des bougies qui s'allument
Quelqu'un monte
Les cloches vont sonner
Un nuage en passant les a fait remuer
A présent on a l'habitude
Personne n'est plus étonné
Les yeux mesurent l'altitude
Où vous êtes placé
Un cœur libre s'est envolé
On peut encore choisir la place
Où l'on pourrait se reposer
Après avoir longtemps marché
Plus bas il reste une surface
Dans la nuit
On écoutait
Serait-ce lui
A l'horizon sans bruit quelqu'un montait au ciel
L'escalier craque
Il est artificiel
C'est une parabole ou une passerelle
L'heure qui s'échappait ne bat plus que d'une aile

# NOCTURNAL ROUND

                    The resonance comes from afar
The worlds draw closer together
On the bell tower's edges cling stars
                Chimneys smoke in the corner
They are candles coming alight
Someone is climbing up
                The bells are about to ring
Stirred by a passing cloud
We are used to it now
                No one is astonished any more
Eyes measure the altitude
                Of your station
A free heart has flown away
                We can still choose our own places
                Where it would be possible to rest
                After walking a long time
Lower down there is one more surface
                        In the night
We were listening
                Perhaps it is he
Soundless on the horizon someone was climbing to the sky
The stairway cracks
                It is an artificial thing
A gangplank or a parabola
Now the escaping hour beats only one wing

## SON DE CLOCHE

                Tout s'est éteint
Le vent passe en chantant
                    Et les arbres frissonnent
Les animaux sont morts
Il n'y a plus personne
                          Regarde
Les étoiles ont cessé de briller
                    La terre ne tourne plus
Une tête s'est inclinée
                        Les cheveux balayant la nuit
Le dernier clocher resté debout
                    Sonne minuit


## SORTIE

Le Vestiaire
                Le Portemanteau
                        La lumière
Au mur des têtes inclinées
                    Un rayon d'électricité
La voix qui chante
                    Un cœur qui s'est ouvert
Dans la salle éclatante
                        Un soir d'hiver
La foule que le feu déverse
Sur le trottoir et sous l'averse
Les diamants renvoyant les éclats
Dans la nuit le silence plane

Et c'est une voiture qui l'emporte

## SOUND OF A BELL

All the lights are out
The wind passes singing
                    And the trees shiver
The animals are dead
There is no one left
                    Look
The stars are not shining now
                    Or the earth turning
A head has bowed
                    Hair sweeps the night
The last bell tower upright
                    Strikes midnight


## EXIT

The Cloakroom
                    The Coatrack
                              The light
Bowed heads on the wall
                    A beam of electricity
The voice singing
                    A heart opened up
In the dazzling room
                    One winter evening
The crowd that the fire pours out
On the sidewalk and under the sudden rain
The diamonds' flashing reply
Silence glides on the night

And a carriage takes all

# AIR

Oubli

porte fermée

Sur la terre inclinée

Un arbre tremble

Et seul

Un oiseau chante


Sur le toit

Il n'y a plus de lumière

Que le soleil


Et les signes que font tes doigts



# POSTE

Pas une tête ne dépasse


Un doigt se lève

Puis c'est la voix que l'on connaît

Un signal

une note brève

Un homme part

Là-haut un nuage qui passe

Personne ne rentre

Et la nuit garde son secret

AIR

      Something forgotten
              closed door
On the sloping earth
A tree trembles
     All alone
         A bird is singing

     On the roof
   All the light left
      Is the sun

And the gestures your fingers make


POST

Not one head sticks over

           A finger is raised
Then comes the voice we know
   A signal
          a short note
  A man goes away
Up there a passing cloud
    No one comes home
And the night keeps its secret

ORAGE

La fenêtre
            Un trou vivant où l'éclair bat
Plein d'impatience
                    Le bruit a percé le silence
On ne sait plus si c'est la nuit
                La maison tremble
Quel mystère
La voix qui chante va se taire
Nous étions plus près
                        Au-dessous
Celui qui cherche
                Plus grand que ce qu'il cherche
Et c'est tout
                Soi
Sous le ciel ouvert
                    Fendu
Un éclat où le souffle est resté
                            Suspendu


MIRACLE

Tête penchée
                Cils recourbés
Bouche muette
Les lampes se sont allumées
Il n'y a plus qu'un nom
                    Qué l'on a oublié
La porte se serait ouverte
Et je n'oserais pas entrer
                    Tout ce qui se passe derrière

On parle
        Et je peux écouter

Mon sort était en jeu dans la pièce à côté

STORM

The window
                A living hole where the lightning beats
Full of impatience
                    The noise has pierced the silence
We no longer know if it's night
                    The house trembles
So mysteriously
The voice that is singing will cease
We were closer
                Underneath
The seeker
            Greater than what he seeks
And that's all
                Oneself
Under the open sky
                Split in two
A brilliance whose flight was left hanging
                                    In the air


MIRACLE

Bowed head
                Upturned eyelashes
Mute mouth
Light now from the lamps
The only thing left is a name
                    They have forgotten
Were the door to open
I would not dare go in
                All that is happening behind

They are talking
            And I can listen
My future was at stake in the next room

## POINTE

Au coin du bois
Quelqu'un se cache
On pourrait approcher sans bruit
Vers le vide ou vers l'ennemi
En tombant la nuit s'est fendue
Deux bras sont restés étendus
Dans l'ombre un regard fixe
                Un éclair éperdu
      Pour aller plus loin vers la croix
Tout ce qu'on voit
      Tout ce qu'on croit
C'est ce qui part
Là ou ailleurs sans qu'on le sache
Avec la peur d'aller trop près
Du ravin noir où tout s'efface

## SECRET

    La cloche vide
    Les oiseaux morts
Dans la maison où tout s'endort
      Neuf heures

La terre se tient immobile
      On dirait que quelqu'un soupire
Les arbres ont l'air de sourire
    L'eau tremble au bout de chaque feuille
      Un nuage traverse la nuit

Devant la porte un homme chante

      La fenêtre s'ouvre sans bruit

## OUTPOST

On the edge of the woods
Someone is hiding
We could making no sound approach
Nearer the abyss or the enemy
As it fell night split apart
Two arms remain extended
In the shadow a fixed stare
                 A flash of frenzied light
     To go on toward the cross
Everything one sees
       Everything one believes
That's what leaves
There or elsewhere and not to our knowledge
With the fear of going too close
To the black ravine where everything is wiped out


## SECRET

     The bell is empty
     The birds dead
In the house where everything is falling asleep
        Nine o'clock

The earth stands immobile
        That sounds like a sigh
The trees look as if they are smiling
        Water trembles at the tip of every leaf
        A cloud moves across the night

In front of the door a man is singing

        The window opens not making a sound

## MINUTE

Il n'est pas encore revenu

Mais qui dans la nuit est entré

La pendule les bras en croix

S'est arrêtée


## BÊTES

Tu regardes en passant l'animal enchaîné
                              Il part de son élan
L'exil entre les haies
          Son. œil sonde le ciel d'un regard étonné
                              La tête contre la barrière
Vers ce reflet de l'infini
                              L'immensité
Prisonnier autant que toi-même
L'ennui ne te quittera pas
Mais je me souviendrai toujours de
                              ton regard
          Et de ta voix
                    terriblement humaine

## MINUTE

He hasn't come back yet

Who has entered the depths of the night

The clock with its arms wide open

Stopped


## ANIMALS

You give a passing glance to the beast in chains
                              His leap is beyond his power
Exile between hedges
      His astonished eyes plumb the sky
                        His head against the bars
Toward that hint of the infinite
                              Immensity
A prisoner just as you are
Boredom will never leave you
But I will always remember
                  the look in your eyes
            And your voice
                  so terribly human

RIVES

La pièce est courte et l'acte est long
As-tu regardé par-derrière

        Le miroir s'enfonçait
On y voyait une ombre
De tous ceux qui sont morts on ne sait plus le nombre
Il y avait un enfant pleurant près d'un ruisseau
Et le vent riant dans les branches
Les feuilles s'envolaient
          Une larme tomba
Quel cri en passant sur la rive
      Faisait frissonner l'eau
Un oiseau
En dessous
     un trou
        l'œil fonce sans limite
Et que trouvera-t-on au bout
 Un paysage fermé
       Une femme endormie
      La toile d'araignée
         Un hamac transparent
Balance un point de plus dans le ciel étoilé

SHORES

The play is short and the act is long
Have you looked at it from behind

                        The mirror was sinking in
With a visible shadow
So many are dead their number who can know
There was a child weeping near a stream
And the wind laughing in branches
Whose leaves were flying away
                        A tear fell down
What cry passing over the shore
                Made the water shiver
A bird
Underneath
            a hole
                    the eye is free to plunge into
And what will be found at the end
A private landscape
                A woman asleep
                The spiderweb
                        A transparent hammock
Swaying one more point in the starry sky

NOMADE

La porte qui ne s'ouvre pas
La main qui passe
Au loin un verre qui se casse
La lampe fume
Les étincelles qui s'allument
Le ciel est plus noir
Sur les toits

Quelques animaux
Sans leur ombre

Un regard
Une tache sombre

La maison où l'on n'entre pas

## NOMAD

      The door that will not open
    The passing hand
          A glass that breaks in the distance
     Smoke from the lamp
And sparks lighting up
       The sky grows dark
        Along the roof tops

Animals here and there
Shadowless

              A look
           A dark spot

The house we do not enter

## LA JETÉE

Les étoiles sont derrière le mur
Dedans saute un cœur qui voudrait sortir
Aime le moment qui passe
        A force ta mémoire est lasse
D'écouter des cadavres de bruits
Dans le silence
        Rien ne vit
Au fond de l'eau l'image s'emprisonne
Au bord du ciel une cloche qui sonne
La voile est un morceau du port qui se détache

Tu restes là
        Tu regardes ce qui s'en va
Quelqu'un chante et tu ne comprends pas
La voix vient de plus haut
        L'homme vient de plus loin
        Tu voudrais respirer à peine
Et l'autre aspirerait le ciel tout d'une haleine

JETTY

      The stars are behind the wall
Inside leaps a heart that would like to go out
Loves the moment passing
           Weary no doubt your memory
Of hearing cadavers of sound
In the silence
        Nothing's alive
The image finds an underwater cell
On the border of the sky resounds a bell
The sail is a piece of the harbor moving away

There you stay
        You watch what is leaving
Someone sings and you don't understand
The voice comes from higher up
            The man from a more distant place
        You aspire to breathe less and less
And the other would draw in the whole sky on one breath

## SILENCE

On parlait encore là derrière
Des hommes passaient deux à deux
C'était peut-être une prière
Qui montait des cœurs du milieu
Entre les murs de la clairière
Une voix qui tinte sur l'eau
L'oiseau prend un autre chemin
Et réveillée par le matin
     La tête sombre
Personne ne connaît le nombre
De ceux qui passent
Entre le mur et le jardin
      Quand le soir devient dur et tombe
       Au loin
On entend le sifflet d'un train


## L'OMBRE DU MUR

Un œil crevé par une plume
Larme qui tombe de la lune
    Un lac
Le monde rentre dans un sac
    La nuit
Les cyprès font le même signe
En blanc la route les souligne
Le paysage hivernal est bleu
      Les doigts tremblent
Deux grands carrés qui se ressemblent
Les ombres dansent au milieu
Des bêtes qu'on ne voit pas
    Des voix

Tout le long du chemin
      Il pleut

## SILENCE

They were still talking there behind
Men were passing in pairs
Perhaps it was a prayer
That rose from the hearts in between
The walls around the clearing
A voice that chimes on the water
The bird goes another way
And awakened by the morning
                          The leaden head
No one can say
How many pass
Between the garden and the wall
                  When evening grows hard and falls
                          Far away
We hear the whistle of a train


## THE SHADOW OF THE WALL

An eye with a quill through its back
A tear that comes from the moon
          A lake
The world finds its home in a sack
          After dark
The cypress trees all give one sign
That the highway's white blank underlines
The hibernal landscape is blue
              Fingers tremble
A big square another resembles
Shadows dance between the two
Invisible animals
          Voices

The length of the road
                  Rain falls

## VEILLÉE

Entre la maison et le ciel
                         Tout se gonfle
Car le vent souffle
Les étoiles montent de la cheminée
Une à une elles se sont fixes
 Sur le fond
                    Une belle troupe
                                          danse
Mais quelques-uns voudraient descendre
On repassera pour vous prendre
                                          Ce soir
Le jour s'était levé plus tard
Une fatigue bien plus grande
Il faudrait rester plus longtemps
                    Nuage qui suit le courant
De la lumière qui s'écaille
Horizon déformé bouche qui bâille


## SOLEIL

     Quelqu'un vient de partir
Dans la chambre
               Il reste un soupir
La vie déserte

     La rue
          Et la fenêtre ouverte
Un rayon de soleil
Sur la pelouse verte

EVENING VIGIL

Between the house and the heavens
                          All balloons
As the wind blows
The stars rise up from the chimney
One by one they stand determined
On the backdrop
                  A handsome troupe
                              dances
But there are those who would like to get down
We will call for you next time around
                              This evening
The sun had arisen later
A much greater fatigue
We would have to stay longer
                  Cloud that follows the tide
Of the scaling light
Distorted horizon mouth yawning wide


SUN

    Someone has just left
In the room
            Remains a sigh
Life deserted

    The street
        And the open window
One ray of sunlight
On the green lawn

EN FACE

　　　　Au bord du toit
　　　　　　Un nuage danse
　　Trois gouttes d'eau pendent à
　　　　　　　　　　la gouttière
　　Trois étoiles
　　　　　　　　Des diamants
　　Et vos yeux brillants qui regardent
　　　　Le soleil derrière la vitre

　　　　　Midi


SENTINELLE

La cheminée garde le toit
Comme le sommet la montagne
Le ciel passe derrière et le nuage bas
Contre l'œil qui regarde
　　　　Minuit
Il reste au fond de l'air encore un peu de bruit
Une sourde chanson qui monte
Ce qu'on entend est plus joli
Les yeux se ferment
　　　　　　On pourrait mourir

　　　　Le reste n'a pas pu sortir
　　A cause de la peur on referme la porte
　　　Cette émotion était trop forte
　　La lueur qui baisse et remonte
　　　　　On dirait un sein qui bat


126

ACROSS THE WAY

On the edge of the roof
A cloud is dancing
Three waterdrops hang from
the gutter
Three stars
Diamonds
And your eyes' brilliance watching
The sun behind the windowpane

Noon


SENTINEL

The chimney keeps watch on the roof
As the summit the mountain
The sky passes behind and the low cloud
Level with the watching eye
Midnight
There is still a little noise in the depths of the air
A muffled song rising
What we hear is more attractive
Eyes close
Death could happen
The rest didn't get out
Because of fear the door has been closed again
That was too strong an emotion
The glow that rises and falls
Like the pulse of a breast

## CIEL ÉTOILÉ

Un arbre orienté vers le ciel
                Cette procession sombre
On éclaire le monde avec des bougies
Tout se tient trop loin et dans l'ombre
Un bruit de pas trouble la nuit

                Le mur se détache lentement
Et son ombre fait une tache
Contre la terre qui descend
Vers la rivière où l'on entend
        Le rire de cristal des roches

Un rayon blanc s'accroche en. haut
        La nuit se balance un moment
Quelque chose tombe dans l'eau
                Une pluie d'étoiles

## JOUEURS

Sa main tendue est une coquille où il pleut
Et l'eau sous la gouttière
                fait un bruit de métal
Derrière le rideau une figure rouge
Dans l'air blanc matinal
        La fenêtre s'ouvre pour parler
Dans la cour le violon grince comme une clef
Et en face de l'homme le mur tient son sérieux
Il pleut sur la tête du joueur
        Il est vieux
Le chien malveillant le regarde
        Et puis c'est un enfant qui court
                Sans prendre garde
                Où il va

STARRY SKY

A tree oriented toward the sky
That somber procession
Candles are all the world's light
Everything keeps its distance and in the shadows
The noise of a footstep disturbs the night

The wall disconnects itself slowly
And its shadow makes a spot
Where the earth is coming down
Toward the river and its sound
The crystalline laughter of rocks

A white light ray hangs from on high
The night for a moment sways
Something falls into the water
A rain of stars


PLAYERS

It is raining in the shell of his outstretched hand
And the water below the gutter
makes a metallic sound
Behind the curtain a ruddy face
In the white early morning air
The window opens to speak
The violin grates in the courtyard like a key
And the wall across from the man refrains from laughing
It is raining on the player's head
He is old
The ill-tempered dog keeps its eye on him
And then there's a child running by
Heedless
Of where he is going

## LE MÊME NUMÉRO

Les yeux à peine ouverts
                 La main sur l'autre rive
Le ciel
        Et tout ce qui arrive
La porte s'inclinait
               Une tête dépasse
Dans le cadre
Et par les volets
On peut regarder à travers
Le soleil prend toute la place
Mais les arbres sont toujours verts
             Une heure tombe
             Il fait plus chaud
Et les maisons sont plus petites
Ceux qui passaient allaient moins vite
Et regardaient toujours en haut
             La lampe à présent nous éclaire
En regardant plus loin
Et nous pouvions voir la lumière
               Qui venait
Nous étions contents
             Le soir


Devant l'autre demeure où quelqu'un nous attend

## THAT NUMBER AGAIN

Eyes scarcely open
   One hand on the other shore
The sky
  And all that happens
The door was leaning down
   A head sticks over
Inside the frame
And the shutters
One can see through
The sun takes up all the room
But the trees are green just the same
    An hour falls
    It's getting warmer
And the houses smaller
The passersby were slowing down
They kept looking upward
    Now we're illuminated by the lamp
Looking further
We could see the light
  Coming
We were happy
   In the evening

In front of the other dwelling where someone awaits us

# AILE

Un souffle sec vient de plus loin
Les ailes noires se balancent
Rien ne part
Au chemin tournant
Les ardeurs du jour se délassent
La maison lourde dort
Les lumières s'éteignent
Dans le jardin deux arbres mourants
Qui s'étreignent
Il parle
Et l'autre pleure
Le soir
Il est onze heures
Et l'oiseau sans forme est parti
L'Ame aux ailes trop courtes
On a détruit le nid
Dans l'air froid quelque chose passe
Un léger bruit monte plus haut
Un rêve prudent qui se cache

WING

A dry breath from further on
The black wings trim their flight
Nothing leaves
On the winding road
The heat of the day relaxes
The heavy house sleeps on
The lights go out
In the garden two dying trees
Embrace
One talks
And the other weeps
In the evening
It's eleven o'clock
And the formless bird has left
The Soul whose wings are too short
They've destroyed the nest
Something passes through the cold air
A slight noise rises higher
A prudent dream going to hide

## RUE

Il faudrait passer là devant
        Paroles que le vent emporte
Combien nous faudra-t-il de temps
Encore une minute et je suis là
        Je reste seul contre la porte
Les arbres auront frissonné
        Si un nuage lourd s'arrête
Devant la porte refermée
Et sous le ciel
        Les heures passent
Moi j'oublierai même mon nom
        Sur le trottoir où ils sont nés
Les oiseaux crient
        D'autres voix roulent
La cloche s'est mise à sonner
        Et toutes les têtes qui tournent
En s'en allant m'auront parlé


## CARREFOUR

S'arrêter devant le soleil
        Après la chute ou le réveil
Quitter la cuirasse du temps
Se reposer sur un nuage blanc
Et boire au cristal transparent
        De l'air
        De la lumière
Un rayon sur le ,bord du verre
Ma main déçue n'attrape rien
Enfin tout seul j'aurai vécu
Jusqu'au dernier matin

Sans qu'un mot m'indiquât quel fut le bon chemin

## STREET

We would have to pass in front
               Words carried off by the wind
How much will be enough time
One minute more and there I am
                   Alone with my back to the door
The trees must have shivered
          If a heavy cloud comes to a stop
In front of the door closed again
And under the sky
          The hours pass by
I'll even forget my own name
           On the sidewalk where they were born
The birds are crying
          Other voices roll on
The bell has begun to ring
          And all the heads that turn
As they leave will have spoken to me


## CROSSROAD

To stop in front of the sun
               After the fall or the waking up
   Once the armor of time is shed
To take a white cloud for a bed
And sip from transparent crystal
        Air
         And light
Gleams on the edge of the glass where
Nothing fills my disappointed hand
So I'll have lived all alone
Up to the final day

Not a word to let me know which one was the right way

## PHARE

Plus loin le verre blanc cassa
Les yeux au plafond se levèrent
Sur le ciel d'aujourd'hui
Un soleil faux qui luit
Un rayon dans la glace
Où mon portrait grimace
A l'envers
Et du grand livre ouvert
L'oiseau qui s'envola
Sortait d'une cage sans porte
De toute la production morte
Du premier jour qui se leva
Au nôtre il n'y a pas de place
Dans mon cœur seul vibre l'espace
Et c'est tout ce qui ne va pas


## EXOTISME

Un profil immortel sur le fronton
A Bornéo ou au-delà
Les rivières sont gelées
Les animaux courent sur la piste
Et le spectateur fou s'amuse
Au concert des Iles Marquises
Le café clair
Elle est bien mise
Elle pose ses bijoux de verre
Et ses mains sont des écrevisses
La paille qu'elles prennent glisse
Chapeau
Bracelets
Faux linon
La musique joue
Je voudrais bien sortir
pour voir si le ciel est encore là

BEACON

            The clear glass broke further on
Eyes rose toward the ceiling
                    On the sky today
A fake sun gleams
                        Bright ray in the mirror
Where my portrait makes a face
                            Wrong way around
And from the great open book
            The bird flew away
Out of a doorless cage
                    For all that has come and gone
                    Ever since the initial dawn
Up to now there is no place
In my heart only vibrates space
        Nothing else is wrong


THE EXOTIC

An immortal profile on the pediment
In Borneo or beyond
                Frozen rivers
The animals race on the track
And the crazy spectator is entertained
At the concert in the Marquesas
                Bright café
She looks very stylish
Arranging her glass jewelry
Her hands are crayfish
The straw that they pick up slips
        Hat
            Bracelets
                    Fake batiste
        The music plays on
I'd like to get out of here
        to see if the sky is still there

## ÉTOILE FILANTE

A la pointe où se balance un mouchoir blanc
          Au fond noir qui finit le monde
          Devant nos yeux un petit espace
                    Tout ce qu'on ne voit pas
               Et qui passe

          Le soleil donne un peu de feu

Une étoile filante brille
Et tout tombe
               Le ciel se ride
Les bras s'ouvrent
                         Et rien ne vient
Un cœur bat encore dans le vide

          Un soupir douloureux s'achève
Dans les plis du rideau le jour se lève


## SOMBRE

Une longue aiguille traverse le rond
Un arbre
                              Un doigt
               La lune borgne
Une fenêtre qui nous lorgne
               La maison fatiguée s'endort
Un appel bref au bord de l'eau
L'argent coule le long des arbres
Ta figure est un bloc de marbre
Où sont passés tous les oiseaux
          La nuit
                         Le bruit
          Quelqu'un fait signe de se taire

On marche dans l'allée du petit cimetière

## SHOOTING STAR

At the point where a white handkerchief sways
        On the black background closing the world
   A blankness in front of our eyes
       Everything we don't see
         That passes by


  A bit of fire from the sun


A shooting star gleams
And everything falls
         The sky is creased
Arms open wide
      And nothing comes
A heart beats on in the empty space


  A painful sigh dies out
In the folds of the curtain dawns the day


## DARK

A long needle crosses the circle
A tree
         A finger
      The one-eyed moon
A monocle-window aimed at us
      The tired house goes to sleep
A brief summons from the water's edge
Along the trees flows silver
Featureless marble your face
Where have the birds all gone
   Night
         Noises
  A finger on someone's lips

On the path of the little cemetery footsteps

## FAUSSE PORTE OU PORTRAIT

           Dans la place qui reste là
Entre quatre lignes
               Un carré où le blanc se joue
       La main qui soutenait ta joue
                   Lune
       Une figure qui s'allume
                   Le profil d'un autre
                           Mais tes yeux
Je suis la lampe qui me guide
Un doigt sur la paupière humide
           Au milieu
       Les larmes roulent dans cet espace
                   Entre quatre lignes
                   Une glace


## VENDREDI TREIZE

La feuille vole cachant l'ombre
               Un jour de plus vient s'ajouter au nombre
Les passants arrêtés à l'étage au-dessus
           Quelqu'un descend
           L'araignée monte
Ou la cage de l'ascenseur
Un oiseau qui ne chante pas parce qu'il a peur
           Un enfant pleure et se résigne
Dans la maison où tout est noir
           Sous la marque du triste signe
Et sur le champ bordé d'espoir
La lumière monte et décline

           Un vœu trop lourd pour le hasard
S'est échappé de ma poitrine

## FALSE PORTAL OR PORTRAIT

In this unmoving square
Inside four lines
A space for the play of white
The hand placed underneath your cheek
The moon
Lights up a face
Another's profile
But your eyes
I am the lamp to guide me
A finger on a moistened lid
In the middle
Tears are rolling through this space
Inside four lines
A mirror


## FRIDAY THE THIRTEENTH

The shadow hidden by a leaf in flight
The total is increased by one day more
The passersby who stopped on the upper floor
Someone goes down
The spider up
Or the elevator cage
A bird who isn't singing out of fright
A crying child gives up its protest
In the house that's all dark
And marked by the sign of sorrow
On the field bounded by hope
Light rises and declines

Too heavy for luck a wish
Escaped from my breast

## CLARTÉS TERRESTRES

Et encore une autre lumière
Le nombre en augmente toujours
Autant d'étoiles que de jours
                    J'attends
Que passe là derrière
La voix qui monte la première
                Le monde regarde à son tour
Le soleil pourrait disparaître
Un astre nouveau vient de naître
                    Eclairant le ciel
Un œil immense artificiel
Qui regarde passer les autres
Avec plus de curiosité
Sur le visage inquiet qui change
                    Un éclair d'électricité

## TERRESTRIAL CLARITIES

And still another light
The number is endlessly increased
As many stars as days
                    I wait
For there to be passing behind
The voice that is the first to rise
                    The world in its turn observes
The sun could disappear
A new star born just now
                    Illuminates the sky
An immense artificial eye
Watching the others pass by
With more curiosity
On its worried changing face
                    A flash of electricity

# DANS LES CHAMPS OU SUR LA COLLINE

Non
          Le personnage historique
Et là le soleil s'arrêtait
C'était un homme qui passait
          Le cheval si maigre
          Qu'aucune ombre ne poursuivait

La neige serait étonnante
          Tout était blanc à quelques pas

Sur tous les animaux qui moururent de froid
          Entre les arbres et la mer
L'eau clapotane
          Le ciel amer
   Resté seul entre les paysans et la lune
Le soir qui descendait devait venir de loin
Lentement la chanson dépassait nos mémoires
          Fallait-il sourire ou y croire
     On attendait
          On regardait
C'est à tout ce qui se passait ailleurs que l'on pensait

## IN THE FIELDS OR ON THE HILL

No
Historical figure
And there the sun was coming to a stop
It was a man passing by
His horse so thin
Not the slightest shadow followed
The snow would be astonishing
A few steps away and everything was white
Over all the animals who died of cold
Between the trees and the sea
Quick lapping water
The bitter sky
Left alone between the peasants and the moon
The evening was coming down and from far away
Slowly the song was leaving our memories behind
Were we supposed to smile or believe it
We were waiting
And watching
Everything happening elsewhere was in our minds

## SURPRISE

Dans la ville il n'y a plus personne
On monte à travers les bois
Quelques-uns tombent
       Et ceux qui arriveront trop tard
C'est toi
           C'est ,moi
La cheminée fume derrière
   Il est resté couché en bas
       Et toi tu, t'agenouilles pour toujours
Il a la tête et le cœur lourds
   Et la chanson est oubliée
         Les heures que l'on a sautées
           À dormir les yeux ouverts
Ne regarde pas ce tableau
C'est une glace brisée
Et ton œil
   ton œil qui n'a pas encore l'habitude


## CALME INTÉRIEUR

        Tout est calme
Pendant l'hiver
      Au soir quand la lampe s'allume
    À travers la fenêtre où on la voit courir
Sur le tapis des mains qui dansent
Une ombre au plafond se balance
     On parle plus bas pour finir
Au jardin les arbres sont morts
Le feu brille
      Et quelqu'un s'endort
   Des lumières contre le mur
Sur la terre une feuille glisse
  La nuit c'est le nouveau décor
Des drames sans témoin qui se passent dehors

## SURPRISE

There is no one left in the city
Climbing up through the woods
A few fall down
      And those who will get there too late
You
        And I
Smoke from the chimney behind
  He is still lying there at the bottom
      And you go down on your knees forever
His head and his heart are heavy
  And the song forgotten
          The hours that we skipped over
         Asleep with open eyes
Don't look at this picture
It's a broken mirror
And your eyes
    your eyes aren't used to it yet


## THE PEACEFULNESS INSIDE

      It's all so peaceful
During the winter
       In the evening when the lamp lights up
    Through the window we see it racing
Over the tablecloth dancing hands
On the ceiling a swaying shadow
      Our voices are lower now
In the garden the trees are dead
The fire sparkles
      And someone falls asleep
    Lights play on the wall
A sliding leaf on the ground
  The setting has changed to night
For disasters no one sees going on outside

## SENTIER

Le vent trop fort ferme ma porte
Emporte mon chapeau comme une feuille morte
Tout a disparu dans la poussière
    Qui sait ce qu'il y a par derrière

Un homme court sur l'horizon
Son ombre tombe dans le vide
Les nuages plus lourds roulent sur la maison
    Le front du ciel inquiet se ride
Il y a des signes clairs au fer de l'occident
Une étoile qui tremble entre les .fils d'argent
Les plis de la rivière qui arrêtera tout
Le monde fatigué s'affaisse dans un trou
     Et du massacre ce qui reste
Se dresse dans la nuit qui change tous les gestes


## MATINÉE

L'ombre penche plutôt à droite
Sous l'or qui luit
Dans le ciel qui fait mille plis
L'air bleu
               Une étoffe irréelle
C'est peut-être une autre dentelle
A la fenêtre
      Qui bat comme une paupière
A cause du vent
   L'air
        Le soleil
           L'été
Les traits de la saison sont à peine effacés

PATH

Too strong a wind shuts my door
Takes off with my hat like a dead leaf
All is lost in the dust
    Who knows what there is behind

A man runs along the horizon
His shadow falls into empty space
The heavier clouds go rolling over the house
    The worried sky wrinkled its brow
There are clear signs in the iron of the west
A trembling star between the silver threads
Folds of the river to make an end of it all
The weary world sinks deep into a hollow
    And what of the massacre remains
Rises up in the night when every gesture changes

MORNING

The shadow leans more to the right
Under the gold gleaming
In a thousand pleats of the sky
The air is blue
                Unheard-of fabric
Perhaps a new kind of lace
At the window
        Beating like an eyelid
Because of the wind
   The air
       The sun
            Summer
The season's features have scarcely been erased

## COULOIR

Nous sommes deux
      Sur la même ligne où tout se suit
      Dans les méandres de la nuit
Une parole est au milieu
      Deux bouches qui ne se voient pas
    Un bruit de pas
Un corps léger glisse vers l'autre
                 La porte tremble
Une main passe
    On voudrait ouvrir
   Le rayon clair se tient debout
   Là devant moi
   Et c'est le feu qui nous sépare
Dans l'ombre où ton profil s'égare
    Une minute sans respire
Ton souffle en passant m'a brûlé

## CORRIDOR

There are two of us
    On the same line where everything follows
    In night's winding ways
Surrounding a word
    The blindness of two mouths
    A sound of footsteps
One weightless body sliding toward the other
            The door trembles
A passing hand
    Why not open
    The ray of clear light stands upright
    Before my eyes
    And it's the fire that comes between us
In the shadow where your profile wanders away
    For a moment not drawing a breath
Yours going by has burned me

# MONTRE

Alors sur le soleil midi devait sonner
               Sur cet immense gong
Un poing lourd s'abattait
Aux applaudissements de tous

Personne n'est resté couché

Les rayons sont déjà debout dans les allées
          Au-dessus de chacun une blanche figure
Tout est noyé dans l'air dans la verdure
Mais quand le soir s'est rallumé
La porte était trop basse
         Et le corps fatigué
Il a fallu traîner son ombre
         Le boîtier s'était refermé
On y lisait un autre nombre
La lune au quart de nuit s'était mise à veiller

## WATCH

Then on the sun was to fall the stroke of noon
$\qquad\qquad\qquad$ On that enormous gong
A heavy fist striking down
Applauded by all

No one has stayed in bed

The light rays are already upright on the paths
$\qquad$ A white face over each one
And everything drowned in the air in foliage
But when evening lit up again
The door was too low
$\qquad$ And the tired body
Had to drag its shadow along
$\qquad$ The watchcase was closed
And there was a different number
The moon on guard at night had begun its vigil

## VISITE

Les bateaux s'étageaient dans le tableau du fond
Où les hommes jouaient aux cartes
Les mots les plus légers montent jusqu'au plafond
Devant eux la fumée s'écarte
Les autres battent des ailes dans les plis des rideaux
L'ennui de la soirée pèse sur les cerveaux
Un livre a refermé ses portes
La prison des pensées où la mienne était morte
Toutes les bouches qui riront
Gagneront la fenêtre et l'air sur le balcon
Les vitres d'en face pâlissent
Dehors tout l'univers résonne
L'heure est venue
                 La cloche sonne
Et tous deux nous nous regardions
Perdus entre les murs de la même maison


## COUVRE-FEU

Un coin au bout du monde où l'on est à l'abri
Les colonnes du soir se tendent
Et la porte s'ouvre à la nuit
Une seule lampe qui veille
Au fond il y a une merveille
Des têtes qu'on ne connaît pas
Au mur des plans qui se ressemblent
Ma figure plus effacée
Entre nous deux l'air chaud qui tremble
         Un souvenir détérioré
Entre les quatre murs qui craquent
      Personne ne parle
Le feu s'éteint sous la fumée

## VISIT

The boats were stacked in the picture on the wall
Where the men were playing cards
The lightest words rise all the way to the ceiling
Pushing aside the smoke
The others beat their wings in the curtains' folds
The evening's tedium weighs down our brains
A book has closed its doors
Prison of thoughts my own lies dead in there
All of the laughing mouths
Will reach the window the balcony fresh air
The windowpanes across the way grow pale
Outside the resonance of the universe
The hour has come
                   At the sound of the bell
The two of us were looking at each other
Lost inside the walls of the same house


## CURFEW

A place of refuge at the end of the world
The pillars of evening reach out
And the door stands open for night
Only one lamp keeps vigil
In the background the wonder
Of unfamiliar faces
The maps on the wall look alike
My own features more effaced
Between the two of us warm trembling air
     A disintegrated memory
Closed inside creaking walls
   No one talks
Smoke smothers the fire

## ENTRE DEUX MONDES

    L'ombre danse
Il n'y a plus rien
Que le vent qui s'élance
Le mouvement s'étend du mur
          Et se gonfle
Il y a des personnages qui naissent
Pour une minute ou pour l'Éternité
La nuit seule qui change
          Et moi-même à côté
      Quelqu'un que le remords tracasse
Sur la route où marque son pas
    On ne voit rien de ce qu'il y a
Le mur seul fait une grimace
      Un signe de mon cœur s'étend jusqu'à la mer
      Personne d'assez grand pour arrêter la terre
Et ce mouvement qui nous lasse
Quand une étoile bleue là-haut tourne à l'envers

## BETWEEN TWO WORLDS

     Dancing shadow
   And nothing at all
   But the spring of the wind
The movement reaches out from the wall
       To grow
Some fictions come to life
For a moment or for Eternity
All that changes is night
         And I close by
   Someone plagued by remorse
On a route where his footsteps leave a trace
  What is there we never see
Only the wall makes a face
    My heart's gesture reaches out to the sea
  Who's big enough to bring the world to a stop
And that movement which makes us weary
When a blue star up there turns in reverse

## VUE D'AUTREFOIS

La cloche qui sonnait au loin
                    Dès le réveil
Battement d'aile
            Sur ma tête où joue le soleil
Un souvenir remue à peine
                Mon cœur s'arrête d'écouter
            Les voix qui parlent
Depuis longtemps tout ce qui s'est passé
Est-ce le même
                En passant qui m'a regardé

Ce sont les mêmes yeux qui tournent
                    Mais le portrait s'est effacé

Les traits de ton visage s'écartent
                    Un autre vient
Le front vieilli qu'avait caché ta main
Enfin la voix qui parle
                Un enfant qui courait ne te rappelle rien
Et celui qui s'en va là-bas
                    Tes lèvres tremblent
Dans un pays lointain et noir
                Tu lui ressembles

## A VIEW FROM LONG AGO

The bell tolling from far away
                    As soon as I was awake
A beating of wings
              On my head where the sunlight plays
A memory scarcely stirs
                My heart stops hearing
            The voices talking
For so long was all that has come to pass
The same
              Passing by with a look at me
Those are the same eyes moving
                But the portrait is effaced
Your features leave their place
            To others
From underneath your hand the aging forehead
And finally your voice
              That running child evokes no memory
There's another in the distance moving away
              Your lips tremble
Through a country remote and dark
            You resemble

## CHAMBRE NOIRE

Un trou dans la lumière et la porte l'encadre
Tout est noir
Les yeux se sont remplis d'un sombre désespoir
                On rit
Mais la mort passe
            Dans son écharpe ténébreuse
            Et dans le sillon creux
                        Une bête peureuse
Qui se débat pour fuir
Vers le fond du jardin où la porte est ouverte
Mais — quelqu'un vient d'entrer
Sans oser dire un mot
La lune est toute gonflée d'eau
Dans la nuit les nuages montent
J'attends l'heure qui sonne
Et je peux écouter
La fin d'un autre conte

## DARKROOM

A hole in the light that the door encloses
Everything's dark
The eyes have filled up with a somber despair
     Someone laughs
But death passes by
    In his shadowy scarf
    And within the hollow furrow
       A timid creature
Struggling to flee
Through the garden toward an open door
But — someone just came in
Not daring to say anything
Water has swollen the moon
Through the night move clouds ascending
I await the striking hour
And I can listen
To another story's ending

## CAMPAGNE

Le champ s'incline à la lumière
Au bas du ciel bleu plus serein
La route court sous la poussière
Mais le soleil n'y est pour rien

La voix qui monte est sans éclat
Un gai refrain dans la voiture
Qui file à l'horizon plus plat
Sur les roues d'orl dans la verdure
Un pan de mur blanc s'élargit
Sous mes yeux qui tournent la meule
Un dernier rayon s'étourdit
Sur le cuivre des tiges molles

Le jour s'est écrasé derrière la maison
Il n'y a plus qu'un trou sous la lampe
Les soucis écartés et même notre espoir
Qui descend plus vite la rampe
Quand la fenêtre allume un feu neuf dans le soir

# COUNTRYSIDE

The field bows to the light
Below the more serene blue sky
Deep in dust the wide road runs
But none of it concerns the sun

The rising voice is lusterless
A gay refrain in the carriage
Rushing along the flatter horizon
On golden wheels through the foliage
Part of a white wall extends
Before my eyes turning the millstone
A last ray of light grows dizzy
On coppery and yielding stems

The day has crashed behind the house
All that's left is a hole under the lamp
The worries set aside and our hope as well
Going more quickly down the ramp
When the window lights up a new fire at nightfall

## PATIENCE

Les voix qui s'élevaient tremblent à l'horizon
Tout est calme dans la clairière
On pourrait voir passer ceux qui s'en vont
Sur cette route sans ornières
D'où vient celui que l'on ne connaît pas
A l'intérieur les gens regardent
Les mains plus vivantes qui passent
Sur celles que l'on ne voit pas
Les mots sont plus lourds que le son
       Ils tombent
Les paupières battent
         On a parlé bas sur ce ton
Et un astre nouveau s'élève
L'espoir luit
          Une porte bouge
          L'arbre d'en face s'est penché
Le mur s'allonge infiniment
            Il n'y a rien de clair dans ma tête
              Sur le trottoir noir et luisant
Toujours le même qui s'arrête

PATIENCE

The voices that were rising tremble on the horizon
All is peaceful in the clearing
A place from which to see those disappearing
Along the rutless road
Whence comes the person we don't know
They are watching from inside
The livelier hands passing over
The ones that can't be seen
Words are heavier than sound
          They fall down
The eyelids flutter
          There was quiet speech in that tone of voice
And a new star rises
Hope shines
          A door makes a move
          Across the way a tree bends closer
The wall endlessly lengthens
          Nothing is clear inside my head
            On the black and shining sidewalk
The same one stops every time

## VISAGE

Il sait à peine d'où tu viens
Malgré la ride qui te marque
Malgré ces traces sur tes joues
Et les mouvements de tes mains
Il ne veut pas que tu t'en ailles
Sur la chaise il n'y a plus qu'un trou
Une forme vague dans l'ombre
Le portrait au fusain dans le coin le plus sombre
Presque rien
Sur le mur quelqu'un passe sa main
Dans les volets le vent se fâche
Tout est fermé jusqu'au matin
Lui doit être loin sur la route


## CORTÈGE

Les mains dressées plus haut touchaient presque le toit
Plus loin les yeux se ferment sur tout ce que l'on voit
La lune au cou tordu les bras sont accrochés
Les arbres sous le vent se hâtent de marcher
Au timbre de ta voix le ciel tiède se vide
Les étoiles perdues tombent dans le ruisseau
Et sur ta main des perles brillent
Pourtant la pluie ne tombe pas
On éteint toutes les fenêtres
Les nuages volent plus bas
La rue se ferme à la tempête
À tous les coups qu'on n'entend pas
Quand le dernier venu franchit la porte basse
C'est derrière le mur le plus épais que tout se passé

## FACE

He scarcely knows where you come from
Despite the wrinkle that brands you
And those lines on your cheeks
And the way your hands move
He doesn't want you to go away
All that's left in the chair is a hole
An indistinct form in the shadow
The charcoal portrait in the darkest corner
Almost nothing
Someone passes his hand over the wall
In the shutters the wind rages
Everything's closed until morning
He must be well on his way by now


## PROCESSION

The hands raised higher were almost touching the roof
Further on eyes close to all that can be seen
The moon has a twisted neck arms hanging on
Making haste beneath the wind go trees
The sound of your voice empties the warm sky
The lost stars are falling into the stream
And on your hand pearls glow
Yet the rain does not fall
They turn off all the windows
The clouds fly nearer the ground
The street is closed to the storm
To all the inaudible blows
When the last to arrive gets through the low door
It's behind the thickest wall that everything happens

## PROJETS

Où iront-ils chercher tout ce qu'il y a
          de grave derrière leurs têtes
Le ciel plisse son front
                    Prépare unè tempête
Les autres sont là pour la fête
Et les astres tendent des fils
De maison à maison
          Les ondes des clochers ébranlent la cloison
Tout est triste plus loin
Et même leurs chansons
          Les hommes fatigués s'étirent
Au jour les lumières pâlissent
   Et sur le trottoir mouillé glissent
          Tous leurs désirs éparpillés
Qui restent morts dans la coulisse
De l'ombre épaisse où ils sont nés


## COURSE

On peut regarder. de travers
Tous ceux qui passent sous l'averse
Les voix qui criaient à l'envers
Et les animaux en détresse
A peine relevés du ciel
Sous les têtes tranchées aux lames des rayons
Quand le soleil fond sur les larmes
Que les yeux perdent leur aplomb
Dans les yeux qu'ils regardent
La chute au fond de la raison
Le tonnerre des voix qui grondent
Sous la voûte éclatante où s'engouffre le monde
La terre était pleine de trous
Le ciel restait toujours limpide
Et les mains cherchaìent dans le vide
L'horizon qui n'existe pas

## PLANS

Where will they look for everything
   that counts in the back of their heads
The sky wrinkles its brow
      Gets a storm ready
The others are there to celebrate
And the stars are stringing threads
From house to house
   The partition rocks under waves from the carillon
It's all sad farther on
And even their songs
   Tired men are stretching
In the daylight lamps grow pale
 And over the wet pavement glide
    All their scattered desires
In the wings behind the depths of shadow
Where they were born they lie dead now


## RACING

One may have one's doubts about
Everyone passing by beneath the downpour
The voices that were crying in reverse
And the animals in distress
Only just now helped up from the sky
Under the heads cut off by blades of light
When the sun hurls itself against tears
And the eyes drop their assurance
Into the eyes they meet
The fall to the depths of reason
The thunder of scolding voices
Beneath the dazzling dome which engulfs the world
The ground was full of holes
The sky was still clear
And hands were searching the emptiness
For the non-existent horizon

# ÉTAPE

Le cavalier mourant levait pourtant sa tête
    Les étoiles le fusillaient
La haie du rêve noir est encore trop épaisse
Nous ne sortirons pas du sort des prisonniers
Mais on peut voir déjà ce qui se passe
Dans les maisons ou sui les toits
Et l'immense bloc où s'entassent
    Même les hommes qui sont là
Les animaux suivent en tas
    La route aux vagues de poussière
Le fleuve où les reflets se noient
    Et les souvenirs qui se meuvent
Dans l'univers refait qui tourne devant toi
    Dans une minute rapide
L'arbre d'en face s'est brisé
Le talus grimpe sur la rive
      Tout le monde s'est incliné
Il faut aller plus lentement
      A cause des plans qui se croisent
      A cause des enterrements
      Et des réveils qui nous déçoivent
      Sous les larmes du firmament

## STOPPING PLACE

The dying horseman managed to raise his head
    Under the fusillade from the stars
The black hedge of dream is still too thick
Whatever happens to captives will happen to us
But already we can see what's being done
In the houses or on the roofs
And piling up on that enormous block
    Even the men who are there
The piles of animals follow
    The wide road with its waves of dust
The river of drowning reflections
    The memories stirring
In the newborn universe turning before your eyes
    In a swift moment
The tree over there has broken
The bank climbs up the shore
        Everyone has bowed
We have to proceed more slowly
        Because of the projects that intersect
        Because of the open graves
        And the disappointment when we open our eyes
        Under the tears of the sky

# ÉCRAN

Une ombre coule sur ta main
La lampe a changé ta figure
La pendule bat
                    Le temps dure
Et comme il ne se passe rien
Celui qui regardait s'en va
            Le monde se retourne et rit
Pour regarder tout ce qui vit


            On marche encore dans le doute
Un tournant au bout de la route
                    Une forêt
Un pont sans arches
            Et la maison où je vivrais
Il faut partir coûte que coûte
Et l'ombre qui passait
            Celui qui regardait
Le monde qui riait
                S'évanouissent
Au fond contre le mur
            Des silhouettes glissent

SCREEN

Over your hand flows a shadow
The lamp has altered your face
The clock is ticking
                    Time remains
And since nothing else is happening
The spectator goes his way
                    The world turns around and laughs
To see all that's alive
                    We go onward still uncertain
At the end of the road there's a turn
                    A forest
A simple bridge
                    And the house where I'd like to live
We must leave just the same
And the passing shadow
                    The man who was looking on
The laughing world
                    Subside
In the background on the wall
                    Silhouettes glide

## ET LÀ

Quelqu'un parle et je suis debout
Je vais partir là-bas à l'autre bout
                    Les arbres pleurent
Parce qu'au loin d'autres choses meurent
                    Maintenant la tête a tout pris

Mais je ne t'ai pas encore compris
Je marche sur tes pas sans savoir qui je suis
Il faut passer par, une porte où personne n'attend
                    Pour un impossible repos
   Tout s'écarte et montre le dos
                    Un peu de vide reste autour
Et pour revivre d'anciens jours
Une âme détachée s'amuse
Et traîne encore un corps qui s'use
Le dernier temps d'une mesure
Plus tenace et plus déchirant
Un chagrin musical murmure

## AND THERE

Someone is talking and here I stand
I'm going to move down there to the other end
                  The trees are crying
Because in the distance other things are dying
                      Now the head has taken it all

But I haven't understood you yet
Wondering who I can be I walk in your footsteps
There is a door to pass where no one waits
               For an impossible lull
    Everything turns its back as it moves aside
                   Where a little emptiness stays
And to relive long-lost days
A soul in its detachment plays
Dragging around its worn-out flesh again
Through the last beats of a measure
More heart rending more tenacious
Murmurs a musical distress

## LA SAISON DERNIÈRE

Un regard
                 ou une grimace
       Le soleil a lui
Dans le miroir ce n'est plus le même
             Un nuage passe à cheval
        En courant le vent le dépasse
Une ombre sur l'œil me tracasse
          Je glisse dans un cauchemar

            Un masque noir
              souligné d'un sourire
         Et celui qui m'entraîne crie
      Il pourrait être mieux ou pire
               et je ris

   Dans la cour il n'y a que moi
Un manteau sombre flotte au-dessus du toit
            Plein de trous
               et quelqu'un m'appelle
Ma paupière est frôlée par un vol d'hirondelle
C'est une main gantée
        Le reste passe derrière les souvenirs
    Mais ce qui est là je pourrais le tenir

Si tu ne regardais pas toujours en arrière

## LAST SEASON

Did someone look
                     or make a face
           The sun lit up
It's another scene in the mirror
                       A cloud on horseback passes by
               The wind rushes to win the race
I'm annoyed by a shadow in my eye
                   And slip into nightmare

                    A black mask
                       a smile underlines
           And dragging me off someone cries
             It could be better or worse
                   to my laughter

  I'm all alone in the courtyard
Above the roof a dark coat floats
                     Full of holes
                         and someone is calling me
My eyelid is brushed by a swallow's wing
It's a hand in a glove
              The rest passes behind the memories
  But what's there I could keep hold of

If you weren't always looking back

## EN BAS

L'éclair passe à travers la bague
Le diamant reste à ton doigt
    La ligne sortait du coin le plus sombre
Celle qui était à son bras formée de l'ombre
avait changé
           La femme souriait
Sous quel jeu de lumière
             La pièce est-elle transformée
Le plafond reste noir
         Voyez sur le balcon
Aujourd'hui les étoiles marchent
          On fait semblant de ne pas voir
Parfois les yeux aussi se lèvent
             Pas si haut
  On pourrait tomber
Le vent qui charge aura tout emporté
Il ne reste plus que la terre
Et ceux qui n'ont pas pu monter

## DOWN BELOW

The flash of lightning passes through the ring
The diamond stays on your finger
     The line was coming out of the darkest corner
The one shadow formed on his arm
had changed
        The woman was smiling
Thanks to what play of light
           Has the room been transformed
The ceiling is still dark
       Look on the balcony
The stars are on the march today
        We pretend not to see
Sometimes our eyes rise too
        Not so high
  We might fall
The charging wind must have carried it all away
Except for the earth
And those who failed in the climb

## TÊTE

Nous ne sommes plus là
                Les autres sont venus
                     Pendant la nuit
Je suis derrière
           Les visages que j'ai connus
Entre les cheminées qui mangent la lumière
Le ciel a grimacé
         Un front soucieux s'est montré

Pendant que nous étions en fête
       Et l'on voyait tourner toutes les têtes
         Que le rire fait éclater
Une lampe s'est allumée
Dans la maison qui ouvre ses fenêtres
Les yeux se sont mis à briller
    Les éclats se brisaient en tombant dans la rue

Et les voix s'élevaient que l'on a entendues
A celle qui restait j'aurais mêlé la mienne
Mais tes yeux se sont refermés
          Et même les persiennes
            Sont retombées

HEAD

We aren't there any more
                              The others came
                                    During the night
I am behind
                  The faces I have known
Between the chimneys eating up the light
A grimace from the sky
                  An anxious forehead appeared

While we were having fun
            And all the heads that laughter
                        Bursts were seen to turn
A lamp went on
As the house opens its windows
Suddenly sparkling eyes
            The scintillations broke as they fell on the street

And the voices we heard began to rise
Except for the one to which I'd have added mine
But once again you've closed your eyes
                        And even the blinds
                                    Have rolled down

## AVANT L'HEURE

Elle est allumée
On ne voit plus qu'elle
        Et le cœur triangulaire
        Qui brille au soleil
Une matinée
Une aube nouvelle
        Mais la journée amère
        Qui reste pareille
Salué en passant quelques yeux inconnus
Où passe le regard que chacun emporte
Et le nom que l'on a cloué
Sur chacune des deux portes
J'ai crié en frappant
           On ne répondait pas
J'ai pleuré en partant
       Mais sans qu'aucun me voie
Et toute la tristesse est restée enfermée
Attendant le soleil qui ouvre les fenêtres
Et les desseins obscurs qui roulent dans ma tête

## BEFORE THE HOUR

All lit up
All anyone can see
      Plus the triangular heart
      Shining in the sun
The new start
Of a morning
      The bitter part
      It's the same old day
Having greeted in passing a few unknown eyes
And the look that passed each one would carry away
With the name they nailed
On both of the doors
I shouted as I knocked
         No one replied
As I left I cried
      But no one could have known
And all the sadness has stayed inside
Waiting for the sun to open the windows
And the shadowy projects rolling around in my mind

## MÉMOIRE

Une minute à peine
                  Et je suis revenu
De tout ce qui passait je n'ai rien retenu
Un point
          Le ciel grandi
                  Et au dernier moment
La lanterne qui passe
              Le pas que l'on entend
   Quelqu'un s'arrête entre tout ce qui marche
On laisse aller le monde
               Et ce qu'il y a dedans
Les lumières qui dansent
               Et l'ombre qui s'étend
Il n'y a plus d'espace
                En regardant devant
Une cage où bondit un animal vivant
La poitrine et les bras faisaient le même geste
Une femme riait
            En renversant la tête
Et celui qui venait nous avait confondus
Nous étions tous les trois sans nous connaître
Et nous formions déjà
              Un monde plein d'espoir

## MEMORY

Scarcely a minute
Before I've come back
Having grasped nothing of all that passed
One point
        The larger sky
              And at the last moment
The lantern going by
           The footstep overheard
  Of all that's in motion someone comes to a stop
Let the world go on as it will
            And everything in it
The dancing lights
           And the spreading shadow
There's more space
             Looking straight ahead
Inside a cage a living animal leaped
With an identical gesture of breast and arms
A woman laughed
          Throwing back her head
And someone mistook the one of us for the other
All three of us were strangers
And formed already
        A world full of hope

BARRE D'AZUR

Les débris culbutés dans le coin
          Il ne reste plus rien
                    Les murs et le triangle
Pourtant
        L'espoir qui nous soutient
L'objet que l'on tient dans la main
   Il fait jour
                    Et l'on marche mieux
La rue est plafonnée de bleu
              Et nos projets sont sans limite
On ne voit pas passer le temps
                Qui va plus vite
                    Dans l'air

Sans savoir si l'on tourne à droite
                Ou à l'envers

NUIT

        Derrière la porte où je suis caché
        Le soir tarde à venir

Je regarde le ciel par cet œil en losange

                Minuit

        Les avions de feu sont presque tous passés
        A travers les signaux d'alarme

        Il y avait dans ma poche une arme

        Une aile qui battait moins haut

        La lune retenant ses larmes

Et des rires moqueurs dans les plis du rideau

A BAR OF AZURE

Debris kicked into a corner
      Nothing remains
           The triangle and the walls
Yet
   Hope sustains us
An object to hold in the hand
  Daylight
         And we walk more easily
The street has a blue ceiling
      And we have no end of plans
We don't see the time passing by
    It goes faster
      In the air

Not knowing if we're to turn right
    Or in reverse


NIGHT

   In my hiding place behind the door
   Evening is slow in coming

Through this diamond-shaped eye there's the sky

        Midnight

   Almost all the warplanes went by
   Straight through the alarm

   In my pocket I had a firearm

   A wing beating now not so high

   Tears that the moon withholds

And mocking laughter in the curtain's folds

# REGARD

Assis sur l'horizon
Les autres vont chanter
Et nous nous avons regardé
La voiture en passant souleva
la poussière
Et tout ce qui traînait retomba
par derrière
Mon œil suivait ainsi
la ligne des ornières
Il s'étirait sans en souffrir
Ton regard le faisait rougir
Et cette voix qui pleure
Sans soulever un souvenir
Est devenue meilleure
Il n'y a plus rien que ton regard
Et devant toi tous ceux qui t'offensèrent

A LOOK

        Seated on the horizon
      The others are going to sing
And as for us we looked on
        The carriage passing by thrust upward
        the dust
        And all that trailed
        fell back down
     My eye following thus
           the line of rust
     Stretched out painlessly
     Your look was making it blush
And that voice full of sorrow
   Not stirring the dust on the past
   Is better now
      And there is nothing left but the look in your eyes
   Facing all those you have reasons to distrust

Selection from

# *Étoiles Peintes*
# *(Painted Stars)*

1921

Collected in *Plupart du Temps*

Translated by

Mary Ann Caws and Patricia Terry

## VIEUX PORT

Un pas de plus vers le lac, sur les quais, devant la porte éclairée de la taverne.

Le matelot chante contre le mur, la femme chante. Les bateaux se balancent, les navires tirent un peu plus sur la chaîne. Au dedans il y a les paysages profonds dessinés sur la glace; les nuages sont dans la salle et la chaleur du ciel et le bruit de la mer. Toutes les aventures vagues les écartent. L'eau et la nuit sont dehors qui attendent. Bientôt le moment viendra de sortir. Le port s'allonge, le bras se tend vers un autre climat, tous les cadres sont pleins de souvenirs, les rues qui penchent, les toits qui vont dormir.

Et pourtant tout est toujours debout prêt à partir.

## LUMIÈRE

Une petite tache brille entre les paupières qui battent. La chambre est vide et les volets s'ouvrent dans la poussière. C'est le jour qui entre ou quelque souvenir qui fait pleurer tes yeux. Le paysage du mur — l'horizon de derrière — ta mémoire en désordre et le ciel plus près d'eux. Il y a des arbres et des nuages, des têtes qui dépassent et des mains blessées par la lumière. Et puis c'est un rideau qui tombe et qui enveloppe toutes ces formes dans la nuit.

## LE MONDE PLATE-FORME

La moitié de tout ce qu'on pouvait voir glissait. Il y avait des danseurs près des phares et des pas de lumière. Tout le monde dormait. D'une masse d'arbres dont on ne distinguait que l'ombre — l'ombre qui marchait en se séparant des feuilles, une aile se dégagea, peu à peu, secouant la lune dans un battement rapide et mou. L'air se tenait tout entier. Le pavé glissant ne supportait plus aucune audace et pourtant c'était en pleine ville, en pleine nuit — le ciel se rattachant à la terre aux maisons du faubourg. Les passants avaient escaladé un autre monde qu'ils regardaient en souriant. Mais on ne savait pas s'ils resteraient plus longtemps là ou s'ils iraient tomber enfin dans l'autre sens de la ruelle.

## OLD SEAPORT

One more step towards the lake, on the docks, before the tavern's lighted door.

Against the wall, the sailor sings, the woman sings. The boats sway, the ships pull a little harder on their chains. Inside there are deep landscapes etched in the glass: clouds are in the room, and the heat of the sky and the sea's sound. All the vague adventures set them to one side. Water and night wait beyond. Soon will come the moment to go out. The port lengthens, the arm stretches towards another clime, all the frames are full of memories, the streets sloping, the roofs about to sleep.

And yet everything always stands upright ready to leave.


## LIGHT

A small spot shines between the eyelids blinking. The room is empty and the shutters open in the dust. The day coming in or some memory sets your eyes to weeping. The landscape of the wall — the horizon behind — your memory in disorder and the sky closer to them. There are trees and clouds, heads protruding and hands wounded by the light. And then a curtain falls and cloaks all these forms in night.


## THE PLATFORM WORLD

Half of everything to be seen was sliding. Near the beacons, dancers and steps of light. Everyone slept on. From a mass of trees of which only the shadow could be seen walking separate from the leaves, a wing freed itself, little by little, tapping the moon in a gentle rapid beat. The air kept to itself entirely. The slippery pavement tolerated no further audacity and yet it was in the middle of town, in the dead of night — the sky holding to the earth in suburban dwellings. The passersby had scaled another world which they gazed at smiling. But no one knew if they would stay there any longer, or if they were finally going to fall into the other way the alley led.

## BLEU PASSÉ

Les mains ouvertes sur la poitrine nue — cette lueur sur le papier déteint, c'est une image. Il y a, derrière, une route qui monte et un arbre qui penche trop, une croix et une autre rangée de branches qui penchent. La pierre des marches s'incline aussi et ce sont des gouttes d'eau qui coulent entre les lignes. La tache qui est au milieu n'est pas une tête — c'est peut-être un trou. Un regard oblique pique le ciel et soutient le trou, la tête. Personne ne parle — personne ne parle d'autrefois. Car plusieurs amis sont là qui se regardent.

## LES MOUVEMENTS À L'HORIZON

Les cavaliers se tiennent sur la route et de profil. On ne sait plus quel est leur nombre. Contre la nuit qui ferme le chemin, entre la rivière et le pont une source qui pleure — un arbre qui vous suit. On regarderait la foule qui passe, elle ne vous verrait pas. C'est une véritable armée en marche ou bien un rêve — un fond de tableau sur un nuage. L'enfant pleure ou dort. Il regarde ou rêve. Le ciel est encombré par toutes ces armées. La terre tremble. Les chevaux glissent le long de l'eau. Et le cortège glisse aussi dans cette eau qui efface toutes ces couleurs, toutes ces larmes.

## MÉMOIRE D'HOMME

De ses épaules larges, contre l'ombre qui danse sur le mur, il tient la place où les autres têtes passeraient. L'instrument est une guitare dont les notes ne vont pas assez haut. Personne n'entend rien, pourtant ses doigts pincent les cordes; il joue et ses pieds battent sans cesse la mesure. Un œil fermé, l'autre perdu derrière le rideau plissé, quand l'air s'étale et que la foule danse, tout le monde danse, tout le monde crie et enfin deux bras blancs sortis des fumées de sa pipe lui entourent le cou. Dans le fond les danseurs arrêtés regardent le tapis.

## PAST BLUE

The hands open on the bare chest — this gleam on the faded paper, is an image. There is, behind, a street rising and a tree leaning too far over, a cross and another row of branches leaning too far over. The stone of the steps slopes also and drops of water run between the lines. The spot in the center is not a head — perhaps a hole. An oblique look prods the sky and sustains the hole, the head. No one speaks — no one speaks of former times. For many friends are there looking at each other.


## MOVEMENTS ON THE HORIZON

The horsemen keep to the road, and in profile. How many they are no one knows any longer. Against the night closing the path, between the river and the bridge a spring weeping, a tree following you. You could look at the crowd passing by without being seen. It's a veritable army marching or else a dream — a backdrop of a painting on a cloud. The child is crying or sleeping. He gazes or dreams. The sky is encumbered by all these armies. The earth shudders. The horses are sliding along the water. And the procession slips by also in this water washing out all these colors, all these tears.


## MAN'S MEMORY

With his broad shoulders, against the shadow dancing on the wall, he takes up the space where the other heads could have passed. The instrument is a guitar whose notes do not resound. No one hears anything, yet his fingers pluck the strings; he plays and his feet keep tapping out the beat. One eye closed, the other lost behind the pleated curtain, when the air spreads out and the crowd dances, everyone dances, everyone shouts and finally two white arms issuing from the smoke puffs of his pipe encircle his neck. In the background the dancers, stilled, are gazing at the carpet.

## LES MUSICIENS

L'ombre et la rue dans le coin où il se passe quelque chose. Les têtes attroupées écoutent ou regardent. L'œil passe du trottoir à l'instrument qui joue, qui roule, à la voiture qui traverse la nuit. Les lames du bec de gaz tranchent la foule et séparent les mains qui se tendent, tous les regards qui pendent et les bruits au hasard. Le peuple est là et tous à la même heure, au carrefour. Les voix qui se dispersent mènent le mouvement sur la corde qui grince et meurt à tous moments. Puis le signe du ciel, le geste qui ramasse et tout disparaît dans le pan de l'habit, du mur qui se dérobe. Tout glisse et le brouillard enroule les passants, disperse les échos, cache l'homme, le groupe et l'instrument.

## AU MOMENT DU BANQUET

Sur les murs de cette salle, où le festin a lieu, les traces de ta vie modeste et fade.

Mais aujourd'hui les paroles sont plus fortes, les gestes sont plus grands, et le bruit plus joyeux.

Les limites de ton cœur s'écartent et peut-être de tous les autres cœurs quelque chose aussi sortira. Mais, sans qu'aucune autre voix s'élève, sans qu'aucun silence tout à coup nous avertisse, les têtes se penchent, les yeux se lèvent et c'est une autre figure dans le cadre que l'on regarde et une autre ligne, du ciel au plafond, qui nous sépare.

## ENTRE DEUX CRÉPUSCULES

C'est dans ce carré de ciel plus clair qu'on allumera les étoiles pour le feu d'artifice. Par-dessus la hauteur des arbres — des mouvements de vent, des bruits d'orage — des appels menaçants. C'est l'endroit où l'on ouvre la grille. Les raies se détachent du mur et c'est une ombre oblique sur la route — qui court trop vite. On attend. Près du bois, d'où sort le pavillon, on entend — et ce sont certainement des pas tranquilles — en même temps que s'élève une prière ou, plus loin, un plus joyeux refrain. Puis le jour entre tout à fait, les cœurs se rétablissent. Puisque tout est encore remis au lendemain.

## THE MUSICIANS

The shadow and the street in whose corner something is happening. The heads, clustered around, listen or look. The eye passes from the sidewalk to the instrument playing, rolling about, to the car traversing the dark. The blades of the gas lamp slice into the crowd, separating the hands outstretched, all the gazes suspended and the chance sounds. The crowd is there, all at once, at the crossroads. The voices dispersing guide the motion along the cord screeching and dying in each moment. Then the sign from the sky. The gathering gesture and everything disappears in a coattail like a snatch of the wall; hiding. Everything is slipping, and fog enfolds the passersby, disperses the echoes, concealing the group, and the instrument.


## AT THE MOMENT OF THE BANQUET

Upon the walls of that room, where the feast takes place, the traces of your modest and colorless life.

But today words are stronger, the gestures more sweeping, and the sound more joyous.

The limits of your heart spread open and perhaps from all the other hearts something will also surge. But without any other voice rising, without any silence warning us suddenly, the heads lean over, the eyes are raised and another figure fills the frame observed, another line, from sky to ceiling, comes between us.


## BETWEEN TWO TWILIGHTS

In this brighter square of the sky the stars will be lit for the fireworks. Higher than the treetops, movements of the wind, sounds of storm — calls with a threat to them. It is the place where the grill is opened. The rays free themselves from the wall, an oblique shadow on the road runs too quickly. People wait. Near the woods, where the pavilion protrudes, people hear — and these are certainly tranquil steps — at the same time that a prayer rises, or, further on, a more joyous refrain. Then the day enters completely, hearts right themselves again. Because everything is once again delayed until the next day.

## APRÈS-MIDI

Au matin qui se lève derrière le toit, à l'abri du pont, au coin des cyprès qui dépassent le mur, un coq a chanté. Dans le clocher qui déchire l'air de sa pointe brillante les notes sonnent et déjà la rumeur matinale s'élève dans la rue; l'unique rue qui va de la rivière à la montagne en partageant le bois. On, cherche quelques autres mots mais les idées sont toujours aussi noires, aussi simples et singulièrement pénibles. Il n'y a guère que les yeux, le plein air, l'herbe et l'eau dans le fond avec, à chaque détour, une source ou une vasque fraîche. Dans le coin de droite la dernière maison avec une tête plus grosse à la fenêtre. Les arbres sont extrêmement vivants et tous ces compagnons familiers longent le mur démoli qui s'écrase dans les épines avec des rires. Au-dessus du ravin la rumeur augmente, s'enfle et si la voiture passe sur la route du haut on ne sait plus si ce sont les fleurs ou les grelots qui tintent. Par le soleil ardent, quand le paysage flambe, le voyageur passe le ruisseau sur un pont très étroit, devant un trou noir où les arbres bordent l'eau qui s'endort l'après-midi. Et, sur le fond de bois tremblant, l'homme immobile.

## TOUT DORT

L'arbre du soir, l'abat-jour de la lampe et la clef du repos. Tout tremble quand la porte s'ouvre sans éveiller de bruit. Le rayon blanc traverse la fenêtre et inonde la table. Une main avance à travers l'ombre, le rayon, le papier sur la table. C'est pour prendre la lampe, l'arbre au cercle étendu, l'astre chaud qui s'évade. Un souffle emporte tout, éteint la flamme et pousse le rayon. Il n'y a plus rien devant les yeux que la nuit noire et le mur qui soutient la maison.

## AFTERNOON

In the morning rising behind the roof, in the shelter of the bridge, in the corner of cypress trees extending past the wall, a cock has crowed. In the bell tower whose glittering peak splits the air, the notes are sounding and already morning noises rise in the only street (not unique) leading from the river to the mountain and parting the wood. A few other words are sought but the ideas are still just as black, just as simple and oddly painful. Little more than eyes, open air, the grass and the water in the background, with a spring or a cool basin at every turn. In the righthand corner, the last house with a larger head at the window. The trees are intensely vital, and all these familiar companions border on the demolished wall, which crashes laughing into the thorns. Above the ravine the sound increases, swells, and if the car passes on the high road you can no longer tell if the flowers or the bells are ringing. Under the ardent sun, when the landscape flames, the traveler crosses the stream on a very narrow bridge, in front of a black hollow where the trees edge along the water napping in the afternoon. And against the backdrop of quivering wood, the man motionless.

## ALL ASLEEP

The evening tree, the lampshade, and the key to rest. Everything trembles when the door opens stirring up no sound. The white beam crosses the window and inundates the table. A hand moves across the shadow, the light beam, the paper on the table. In order to take the lamp, the tree stretched out in the circle, the hot star escaping. A breath whisks all away, quenches the flame, pushes the beam aside. There is nothing more before the eyes but pitch-black night and the wall holding up the house.

## MOUVEMENT INTERNE

Sa face écarlate illumine la chambre où il est seul.
Seul avec son portrait qui bouge dans la glace. Est-ce
bien lui? Serait-ce l'œil d'un autre? Il n'en aurait
pas peur. Son pied manque le sol et il avance en
éclatant de rire. Il croit que cette tête parle — celle
qu'il a devant lui, ivre, les yeux ouverts. Le plafond
s'abaisse, les murs vont éclater et il rit. Il rit au feu
qui lui chauffe le ventre; à la pendule qui bat
comme son cœur. La chambre roule — ce bateau
dont le mât craquerait s'il faisait plus de vent. Et,
sans s'apercevoir qu'il tombe, sur le lit où il va
s'endormir, il croit encore rêver que les vagues l'emportent.
Trop loin. Il n'y a plus rien que le rire
idiot du réveil et le mouvement inquiétant de la porte.

## TUMULTE

La foule descendait plus vite et en criant. Ils venaient tous du fond, de derrière
les arbres, de derrière le bois du cadre, de la maison. Chaque visage blanc avait
un regard animé — et sur leurs traces les paroles plus lourdes s'effaçaient. Au
bruit qui se fit dans le coin]e plus sombre tout s'arrêta, tout le monde s'arrêta,
même celui dont les yeux étaient tournés vers la muraille. Et alors, à cause du
vent, les fleurs de la tapisserie et des étoffes remuèrent.

INTERNAL MOVEMENT

   His scarlet face lights up the room where he is alone.
Alone with his portrait which stirs in the mirror. Is this
really himself? Could it be someone else's eye? He wouldn't be
afraid of it. He misses his footing, and goes on with a burst of
laughter. He thinks the head is talking — the one there in front
of him, drunken, its eyes open. The ceiling gets lower, the
walls are going to explode, and he laughs. He laughs
at the fire warming his belly; at the clock, beating like his
heart. The room is rolling — a ship whose mast would crack in a
higher wind. And; without realizing he is falling, on the bed
where he will fall asleep, he thinks he is dreaming again that the
waves are carrying him off. Too far. There is nothing left but
the idiot laughter of the alarm clock and the disquieting motion
of the door.

TUMULT

Shouting, the crowd was rushing down. They all came from the depths, from be-
hind the trees, from behind the wooden frame, of the house. Each white face
looked animated — and along their path the most substantial words were quieted.
At a sound from the darkest corner, everything stopped, everyone stopped, even
one whose eyes were turned toward the wall. And then, the flowers of the tapestry
and of the fabrics stirred in the wind.

*Mary Ann Caws*

## CIEL OUVERT

Le fil descend. Du haut du ciel le fil descend, lourd, droit, noir — descend sur le sommet de la tête nue — la tête du vieillard qui s'arrête. Il est dans un jardin bordé de grilles, en cage et le monde est autour. Les autres gens tournent autour, le long des arbres. Le temps est lourd, les yeux, les étincelles éclairent la nuit noire ou la lueur du film — cette lueur qui n'est pas encore dans sa tête. Un nuage de suie se gonfle, avalanche de coton sans eau, la maison se gonfle aussi, la poitrine, les arbres se gonflent et la tête est perdue. La peau — sous les tiges de feu — ruisselle — et l'eau s'écarte de la masse d'huile qui glisse, qui joue — les gonds de la plus grande porte qui tourne. Le ciel fendu — le fil descend — l'éclair. Le monde à sa lueur est à peine entrevu.

## OPEN SKY

The thread comes down. From the top of the sky the thread comes down, heavy, straight, black — comes down on the top of the bare head — the head of the old man who stops. He is in a garden bordered by railings, in a cage, and the world is around. The other people walk around, close to the trees. The weather is heavy, and eyes, sparks brighten the pitch-black night or the glow of the film — that glow which is not yet in his head. A cloud of soot expands, an avalanche of dry cotton, the house expands too, the chest and the trees expand, and the head is lost. The skin — under the stalks of fire — streams — and the water moves away from the mass of oil slipping and playing — the hinges of the largest door turning. The cloven sky — the thread coming down — the flash. Barely a glimpse of the world in its glow.

*Mary Ann Caws*

Selection from

# *Cravates de Chanvre (Ties Made of Hemp)*

1922

Collected in *Plupart du Temps*

Translated by Mary Ann Caws

## TEMPS COUVERT

Je suis au milieu d'un nuage
de neige
ou de fumée
L'éclat du jour fait son tapage
la fenêtre en battant
ouvre le mur du coin
la paupière assoupie
et l'œil déjà baissé
Plus loin
sur le détour où aurait dû tomber
le grand vent qui passait
en roulant l'atmosphère
la neige et la fumée
Quelques grains de soleil
et le poids de la terre
à peine soulevée

## DULL WEATHER

I am in the middle of a cloud
                        of snow
                    or of smoke
The daybright is making its commotion
                            the window clacking
                            opens the corner wall
the eyelid drowsing
                        and the eye already lowered
            Further on
the detour where the great wind passing
                    should have fallen
                        wheeling the atmosphere
                        the snow and the smoke
A few seeds of the sun
                    and the weight of the earth
        scarcely lifted

## LA LANGUE SÈCHE

Le clou est là
    Retient la pente
Le lambeau clair au vent soulevé c'est un souffle
                  et celui qui comprend
      Tout le chemin est nu
les pavés les trottoirs la distance le parapet sont
                     blancs
        Pas de goutte de pluie
        Pas une feuille d'arbre
        Ni l'ombre d'un habit
J'attends
      la gare est loin

la terre se dessèche
tout est nu tout est blanc

Avec le seul mouvement déréglé de l'horloge

le bruit du train passé
          J'attends

## DRY TONGUE

The nail is there
      Holding back the slope
The bright tatters raised in the wind a breath
                  and one who understands
      The whole path is naked
the pavement the sidewalks the distance the parapet are white
           Not a drop of rain
           Not a leaf
           Not the shadow of a garment
                  I am waiting
                    the station is far off
However the river runs from the wharves upstream
      the land is drying out
         all is naked all is white
With the single crazed movement of the clock
      the sound of the train gone by
         I am waiting

Selection from

# *Grande Nature*
# *(Great Nature)*
1925

Translated by Mary Ann Caws

## DÉTRESSE DU SORT

J'interroge la porte ouverte
                    sur le mur blanc
J'interroge le toit
                    Et le champ incliné
                    derrière la maison
Une main enveloppe la terre entre ses doigts et la lance aux
diverses couleurs du ciel qui est ici d'un roux de lièvre
        Tous les autres animaux détalent vers l'orient
        plus bas
        Seul je reste regardant en l'air venir des véhicules
        pleins par des chemins encore impraticables
L'hiver ce sont des torrents où l'on entend sombrer des
bateaux en détresse et gémir le chœur des naufragés
        Cependant nous sommes encore assez loin de la mer
Une suite de collines entoure le creux où l'on voit se perdre
les signaux des lampes d'équipage
        Des chiffres énormes sont inscrits sur les arbres et peu
        à peu des canots s'avancent sur les lames pour venir
        prendre le signal qui part du phare
À ce point culminant c'est un oiseau qui se perche
        et qui chante


        Et sa parole a pris le sens du vent
                        la direction des îles
Mais aucun geste de menace ne le ferait partir

                    *
                *       *

L'Arc qui entour ce paysage sinistre et désolé
perd sa couleur
                    Je crois qu'il s'use
                    *
                *       *

Et si tout ce que j'ai vu m'avait trompé
S'il n'y avait rien derrière cette toile
qu'un trou vide


212

## DISTRESSED FATE

I question the door opened
          On the white wall
I question the roof
          And the field sloping
          behind the house
A hand folds up the earth between its fingers
 and hurls it to the various colors of the sky
 here the russet of a hare
          All the other animals light out towards
    the east lower down
          I alone remain watching in the air
    as the full cars move along these roads
    still undriveable
In winter there are torrents where you hear
      boats sinking in distress and the chorus of the
      shipwrecked moaning
      However we are still far enough from the sea
A series of hills surround the hollow where you see
      the signals of the running lamps disappearing
Enormous figures are inscribed on the trees
      and little by little canoes move forward on the
      waves coming to take the signal leaving from the
      lighthouse
      At this high point a bird perches singing
      And his song has taken the direction of the wind
                  the direction of the
                islands
But no menacing gesture would make it leave

          *

        *    *


The Arch surrounding this sinister and desolate
landscape is losing its color
          I think it's wearing out.

          *

        *    *

Ce qui me rassure un peu c'est que je pourrais toujours
    me retenir aux bords
Garder la rampe
Et laisser sur la terre un léger souvenir
Un geste de regret
Une amère graimace
        Ce que j'aurai mieux fait

And if all I've seen had deceived me
If there were nothing behind this canvas
    but an empty hold
What reassures me a bit is that I could always
hold to the sides
Keep to the ramp
And leave on the earth a slight memory
A gesture of regret
A bitter grimace
            What I'll have done best

## CE SOUVENIR

Je t'ai vu
Je t'ai vu au fond devant le mur
J'ai vu le trou de ton ombre sur le mur
Il y avait encore du sable
Et tes pieds nus
La trace de tes pieds qui ne s'arrêtait plus
Comment t'aurais-je reconnu
Le ciel tenait tout le fond tout l'espace
Un peu de terre en bas qui brillait au soleil
Encore un peu de place
Et la mer
L'astre est sorti de l'eau
Un navire passait volant bas
                    Un oiseau
La ligne à l'horizon d'où venait le courant
Les vagues mouraient en riant
Tout continue
On ne sait pas où finira le temps
                    Ni la nuit
Tout est effacé par le vent
            On chante autrement
            On parle avec un autre accent
Je reconnais des yeux qui sont restés vivants
Et la pendule qui sonnait dans la chambre
Une heure en retard
Le matin vert qui vient quand on n'a pas dormi
Il y a un gai ruisseau d'eau claire et d'autres cris
Devant la porte une sijhouette qui disparaît
Un visage dans la lumière
Et au milieu de tout ce qui vit et se réveille
La même et seule voix qui persiste
dans mon oreille

## THIS MEMORY

I saw you
I saw you back there before the wall
I saw the hole your shadow left on the wall
There was still some sand
And your bare feet
The trace of your feet which kept on and on
How should I have recognized you
The sky took all the depth all the space
A little land below shining in the sun
A little room left
And the sea
The star has emerged from the water
A ship was passing flying low
                  A bird
The horizon line from which the current came
The waves were dying laughing
Everything goes on
We don't know where time will end
                Or night
Everything is rubbed out by the wind
             People sing differently
             People speak with another accent
I recognized still living eyes
And the clock that sounded in the room
An hour late
The green morning coming when we haven't slept
There's a gay stream of clear water and other cries
Before the door a silhouette disappearing
A face in the light
And in the middle of all that lives and wakes
The same and single voice persisting
in my ear

Selection from

# *La Balle au Bond*
# *(Rebounding Ball)*
## 1928

Translated by

Mary Ann Caws and Patricia Terry

## COURTE VIE

On va plus loin que la ligne arrêtée un jour au bord du sol. C'est le chemin fantasque qui tourne vers la voûte abritée dans un coin bleu et vert; miracle d'un habit mal fait, mis à l'envers, au dos d'un autre. La tête s'incline trois fois. De loin le genou plie et la main se soulève. Le gant blanc est fané, la feuille se détache. Le vent, comme un cheval emballé, s'abat sur le couchant, couvert d'écume, et le soir s'assombrit. Les voix courent devant et le fleuve sourit, quand les tristes lanternes, le long du quai, s'allument. L'heure pleine est passée sur une autre qui sonne. Les pas des voyageurs courent déjà plus loin. Moi, j'espère toujours que le ciel me pardonne. Mais je suis trop pressé des conseils qu'on me donne pour racheter mon temps.


## CHAMP CLOS

Il y a sur la chambre vide une auréole. Les plantes
qui bordent les franges du toit jusqu'aux racines
et même les feuilles blondes apportent l'ombre.

Le quatrième mur va plus loin. Plus loin que l'angle
où le rideau soupire. Plus haut que la nuit noire et
la fumée mouvante de l'usine. On chante à côté de
la chambre vide, contre le toit près de l'étoile.

Il y a une auréole qui n'est pas la lune, une lumière
qui n'est pas la lampe. Mais un carré noir sur la
terre sombre.

Et ce carré, la chambre vide.

## BRIEF LIFE

Going further than the line stopped one day at the field's edge. It's the odd path turning towards the vault sheltered in a corner blue and green; miracle of a poorly made suit, put on the wrong way round, on the back of another. The head bows thrice. Far off, the knee bends, and the hand is raised, the white glove is faded, the leaf comes off. The wind swoops down upon the west, like a dashing horse flecked with foam, and the evening grows darker. Voices drift ahead and the river smiles, when the sad lanterns along the wharf light up. The hour at its fullest has passed by, over another, resounding. The travelers' steps are already hurrying further along. I am still hoping the heavens will pardon me. But I am too beset with advice given me to redeem my time.


## CLOSED FIELD

There is a halo on the empty room. The plants edging the fringes of the roof, down to the roots, and even the blond leaves contribute shade.

The fourth wall goes further. Further than the corner where the curtain is sighing. Higher than the black night and the factory's shifting smoke. Beside the empty room someone is singing, against the roof, close to the star.

There is a halo which is not the moon, a light which is not the lamp. But a black square on the somber earth.

And this square, the empty room.

## UN HOMME FINI

Le soir, il promène, à travers la pluie et le danger
nocturne, son ombre informe et tout ce qui l'a fait amer.

A la première rencontre, il tremble — où se réfugier
contre le désespoir?

Une foule rôde dans le vent qui torture les branches,
et le Maître du ciel le suit d'un œil terrible.

Une enseigne grince — la peur. Une porte bouge
et le volet d'en haut claque contre le mur; il court
et les ailes qui emportaient l'ange noir l'abandonnent.

Et puis, dans les couloirs sans fin, dans les champs
désolés de la nuit, dans les limites sombres où se
heurte l'esprit, les voix imprévues traversent les
cloisons, les idées mal bâties chancellent, les cloches
de la mort équivoque résonnent.

## AU BOUT DE LA RUE DES ASTRES

Les lunettes s'inscrivent exactement dans la forme nouvelle
du ciel. Les deux figures se rapprocheraient-elles pour regarder?
La lune et le soleil attendent en gardant la distance.

Cependant les heures tombent plus lourdes et plus longues
qu'autrefois.

Puis, ce sont des paupières qui se ferment, des nuages qui passent.

Et un moment de calme et de repos pour nous qui marchons
depuis si longtemps. A un signal donné, une main plus fine, aux
ongles rouges, soulève un rideau qui arrêtait le jour. Et l'on voit
les rayons qui dorment. L'eau qui flotte sur l'herbe. Le numéro.
Et la rue, où ne passe personne, enveloppée dans un grand
manteau noir qui, de temps à autre, se déplace.

## A FINITE MAN

In the evening, through the rain and nocturnal danger, he walks his shapeless shadow and all that has made him bitter.

At the first encounter, he trembles — where to take refuge against despair?

A crowd prowls in the wind tormenting the branches, and the Master of the sky follows him with a terrible eye.

A signboard is creaking — fear. A door moves and the shutter high above clacks against the wall; he runs and the wings which were bearing the black angel away abandon him.

And then, in the endless corridors, in the desolate fields of night, in those somber limits the mind collides, unexpected voices cross the partitions, the poorly constructed ideas lose their balance, the bells of equivocal death are tolling.

## AT THE END OF THE STREET OF STARS

The spectacles are exactly inscribed in the sky's new form. Would the two figures come nearer to see? The moon and the sun are waiting, keeping their distance.

Meanwhile the hours are falling heavier and longer than ever before.

Then, eyelids are closing, clouds passing.

And a moment of calm and repose for us; we have been walking for so long. At a given signal, a more delicate hand with red fingernails lifts a curtain which kept out the day, and the light beams are seen sleeping. Water floating on the grass. The number. And the street, where no one passes, wrapped in a large black cloak, shifting from time to time.

*Mary Ann Caws*

## LE TEMPS PASSE

La première étoile allumée dans le ciel est déjà
reflétée sur la vitre de la cabane. Le voyageur, sur la
route trop longue, sans une pierre pour s'asseoir,
sans un arbre où s'abriter de la nuit trop vaste et des
bruits qui venaient de si loin, fuyait devant les
menaces vagues de la peur.

Il ne trouvait jamais d'autre abri que l'espace.
La lumière était descendue peu à peu, aux angles de
la croix, au sommet du calvaire et contre les marches
délabrées qui s'éboulent dans un fossé de carrefour
où commence le chemin qui monte. Il voyait la
trace lumineuse des pas d'un autre qui était resté là
pendant longtemps. Celui qui est toujours parti quand
on l'attend.

## L'ANGOISSE

Des paroles confuses s'élèvent, dans la nuit. Et des mains restent tendues
vers la lumière. Dans la chambre où l'on craint de mourir, la porte refermée, on
n'entend plus de bruits. La prière est inconnue aux habitants de l'ombre. Et leurs
lèvres, comme leur cœur, restent muettes.

De la rue, monte un murmure paisible. Le soir est tiède. Alors l'espoir renaît.
Mais les murs trop étroits se serrent. Ils garderont longtemps la trace significative
de ces nombres. Et même, pour plusieurs, jusqu'à leur nom.

## TIME IS PASSING

The first star lit up in the sky is already reflected upon the
windowpane of the hut. The traveler, too long on the road, without
a stone to sit upon, without a tree for shelter from
the night too vast and the sounds coming from so far off, fled
before the vague threats of fear.

He never found any other shelter but space. The light had come
down little by little, at the angles of the cross, on top of the
calvary and against the dilapidated steps sinking into a ditch at
the crossroads where the rising path begins. He saw the luminous
trace of the steps of another who had remained there for a
long time. The one who has always left when you are waiting
for him.

*Mary Ann Caws*


## ANGUISH

In the night, confused words are rising. And hands are still reaching out to-
ward the light. In the room with its door closed again, where someone is afraid
of dying, no more sounds are heard. Prayer is unknown to the inhabitants of
shadow. And their lips, like their hearts, remain silent.

From the street there rises a quiet murmuring. The evening is warm. Then
hope is reborn. But the walls, too narrow, close in. They will long retain the
meaningful trace of these figures. And even, for many, their names.

## QUAND ON N'EST PAS DE CE MONDE

Il y eut, tout le temps que dura l'orage, quelqu'un qui parla sous le couvert. Autour de la lumière que traçait son doigt sur la nappe on aurait pu voir de grosses lettres noires, en regardant bien. Bientôt ce fut un autre ton. Et la couleur du Mur changea. La voix semblait venir de derrière. On ne savait pas si c'était le mur ou le paravent. Les lettres disparurent ou plutôt elles s'étaient réunies et formaient un nom étrange qu'on ne déchiffrait pas.


## LA PAROLE

Si la lumière s'éteint, tu restes seul devant la nuit. Et ce sont tes yeux ouverts qui t'éclairent.

Du jardin, montent des bruits que tu n'écoutes pas. De la rouille des feuilles et des branches, l'eau court jusq' au matin, et elle change. de voix. Et, tout à coup, tu penses au portrait blanc qu'encadre la fenêtre. Mais personne ne passe et ne regarde. Et pas même le vent ne vient troubler les arbres, animer cette immobilité et ce silence où ton esprit blessé se relève et tournoie.


## PORT

La longue avenue, le ciel gris et les derniers étages, avec des têtes plus pâles qui montent le long du parapet. La petite maison figure assez bien le cottage. La rue s'enfonce entre les murs profonds et au bout du pont tourne le phare. La jetée arrondit son bras autour de l'eau. La lune avale lentement les étoiles. Et l'écume avec ses rayons.

La sirène des bateaux du fleuve déchire les rideaux devant l'hôtel qui ouvre ses fenêtres et tous les voyageurs attendent le départ. Quelques marins dansent avec les réverbères. On entend la musique dans les rochers du port. Peu après le gouffrç se déplace. Et la voile triangulaire avance en déployant le jour.

## WHEN ONE IS NOT OF THIS WORLD

There was, all the time the storm lasted, someone speaking under cover. Around the light his finger traced on the tablecloth, large black letters would have been visible to anyone looking hard. Soon the tone was different. And the color of the wall changed. The voice seemed to come from behind, whether the wall or the screen, no one knew. The letters disappeared or rather they had merged, forming a strange and undecipherable name.

*Mary Ann Caws*

## THE WORD

If the light goes out, you remain alone confronting the dark. And your eyes, open, illuminate your way.

From the garden arise sounds which you do not hear. From the redness of the leaves and the branches, the water runs toward the morning, changing voice. And suddenly you think of the white portrait framed by the window. But no one goes by or even looks. Not even the wind comes troubling the trees, to quicken this immobility and this silence where your wounded spirit lifts and circles.

## PORT

The long avenue, the gray sky, and the highest floors, with paler heads rising the length of the parapet. The little house looks rather like a cottage. The street plunges between the deep walls and at bridge end, the lighthouse turns. The jetty clasps its arms about the water. Slowly the moon swallows in its rays the stars and the foam.

The mermaid of the riverboats thrusts apart the curtains across from the hotel, opening its windows; all the travelers await the hour to leave. A few sailors dance about with the gas lights. In the rocks of the port, music is heard. Just afterwards, the abyss moves to the side. And the triangular sail advances, unfolding day.

## LE SOMMEIL DU CŒUR

De ses ongles il griffait la paroi dure de cette cage. Il était prisonnier du cauchemar ou de ses ennemis.

On marchait au dehors. Une main qui cherchait la sienne le frôla. Plus fraîche que l'aube sur son front. La fenêtre s'ouvrait au vent trop fort qui roulait sur les toits. C'était encore la nuit.

Et sa poitrine libre respirait un air frais qui changeait le décor. Mais, dans sa mémoire persiste un mauvais souvenir. Et il y a aussi le nom de celui qui était la cause de ce rêve.


## FLAMMES

L'eau et la clarté de la lune lui coulaient doucement dans l'œil.

Les derniers passants de la nuit traînaient leur sommeil sur le marbre. La couleur se mêlait au bruit. Du haut de la pente, le roulement des rêves glisse avec des éclairs. Dans un champ dévasté où se perdent des ombres, un cheval saute une haie d'étincelles. Une écharpe nocturne s'accroche aux étriers de ce cavalier bleu. Une foule irréelle s'engouffre sur le trottoir d'en face, au milieu des reflets du mur trempé de pluie que suivent les personnages imaginaires des affiches.

## HEART ASLEEP

With his nails he scratched on the hard wall of this cage, a prisoner of the nightmare or of his enemies.

Outside, someone was walking. A hand, seeking his, brushed against him. Cooler than the dawn upon his forehead. The window opened to the wind, rolling over the roofs and too strong. It was still night.

And his chest freely breathed a fresh air altering the surroundings. But in his mind a bad memory lingers. And also the name of the one person provoking this dream.

## FLAMES

Water and the moon's brightness flowed gently into his eye.

The night's last passersby dragged their sleep along the marble. Color mingled with sound. From the top of the slope, the rumbling dreams slip about and flash. In a devastated field where shadows are lost, a horse jumps a hedge of sparks. A nocturnal scarf catches on the spurs of this blue horseman. An unreal crowd is engulfed on the opposite sidewalk amid the reflections of the rain-soaked wall followed by the glances of the imaginary figures of the posters.

*Mary Ann Caws*

Selection from

# *Flaques de Verre*
# *(Pools of Glass)*
1929

Translated by Mary Ann Caws

## ÇA

Les quelques raies qui raccourcissent le mur sont des indications pour la police. Les arbres sont des têtes, ou les têtes des arbres, en tout cas les têtes des arbres me menacent.

Elles courent tout le long du mur et j'ai peur d'arriver à l'endroit où l'on ouvre la grille. Sur la route mon ombre me suit, oblique, et me dit que je cours trop vite. C'est moi qui ai l'air d'tin voleur. Enfin, près du petit bois d'où sort le pavillon, je vais crier, je crie mais des pas tranquilles me rassurent. Et quelqu'un vient m'ouvrir. Par la porte j'aperçois des amis qui sont en train de rire.

Peut-être est-il question de moi?


## ...S'ENTRE-BAILLE

Du triangle des trottoirs de la place partent tous les fils et la faux de l'arc-en-ciel, brisée derrière les nuages.

Au milieu celui qui attend, rouge, ne sachant où se mettre.

Tout le monde règarde et c'est au même endroit que le mur découvre sa blessure.

La main qui ferme le volet s'en va, la tête que coupe le rayon ne tombe pas — et il reste cette illusion qui attirait, au même instant, tous les regards vers ce drame qui se jouait, face au couchant, sur la fenêtre.


## LE PAVÉ DE CRISTAL

A côté, un mouvement léger trouble les murs.

Dans cette chambre bleue, sans porte ni fenêtre, une lampe s'allume nuit et jour.

Sur la table on entend courir les mains — le bruit s'allonge — et le temps passe autour, sans rien changer.

Et maintenant quelqu'un arrive, quelqu'un attend sur le palier.

Celui qui s'arrête et écoute — celui qui vit tout seul dans la chambre à côté.

## THAT

The several streaks shortening the wall are indications to the police. The trees are heads, or the heads of trees, in any case, the heads of trees threaten me.

They run the length of the wall and I am afraid of arriving at the place where the grating is opened. On the road my shadow follows me, oblique, and informs me I am running too fast. I am the one who looks like a thief. Finally, near the little wood where the pavilion can be seen, I am about to scream, I scream, but calm steps reassure me. And someone comes to open the door; through it I see some friends laughing.

Perhaps it is about me?


## ...SLIGHTLY OPEN

From the triangle of the sidewalks on the square start all the threads and the rainbow's scythe, broken behind the clouds.

In the center, crimson, he waits, not knowing where to put himself.

Everyone is looking, and just in that place the wall uncovers its wound.

The hand closing the shutter moves  away, the head severed by the light beam does not fall — and this illusion remains attracting all the gazes at once towards this drama, played out upon the window, facing the setting sun.


## THE CRYSTAL PAVEMENT

To one side, a slight motion disturbs the walls.

In this blue room without door or window, a lamp is lit night and day.

Over the table, hands are heard running — the sound extends — and time passes about, changing nothing.

And now someone arrives, someone awaits on the landing.

He who stops and listens — who lives all alone in the room to one side.

## L'ÉLAN NORMAL

Derrière chaque tête, des notes de clairon, un éclair de lampes électriques.

Les jambes, les bras, les muscles du visage s'agitent et rendent le personnage absolument méconnaissable.

Puis le silence bas, la nuit, la vérité.

Devant chaque tête un masque blanc, un mot pour rire, l'âme immobile.

L'œil s'attarde sur chaque trait, sur la ligne limpide et le corps tout entier.

Le calme froid.

Et, en même temps, sans que personne au monde le leur dise, des mots confus se mettent à sortir.

Les lèvres tremblent.

Tout ce qui peut mentir va arriver.


## L'ÂME ET LE CORPS SUPERPOSÉS

Dans la chambre l'esprit malade et le corps allongé.

La flamme perce.

Le triangle de la lampe s'oriente au plafond selon le sens de la pièce à côté.

Quand tous les désespoirs se mettent en travers, que la route est barrée.

Quand on n'espère plus qu'en la dernière goutte, la dernière heure, la chaîne relevée.

J'observe le triangle d'un œil distrait par la fièvre et par les battements du cœur qui guide le danger.

Sur le mur opposé au côté de la glace — le gouffre noir, gelé où règnent le vide et le silence menaçants, la possibilité de toutes les morsures — m'apparaissent les paysages réjouis et souriants de rayons de soleil, de cloches lumineuses, de cris filant le long, de couleurs détachées, de trombes claires sur un ciel trop chargé.

Mais dans l'ovale qui tient le visage tout entier immobile et la mémoire inquiète, trouée, usée par les efforts retenus à jamais — on a précisément la notion du temps qui se remet, de celui qui arrive et la limite de nos mouvements en désordre dans cet espace étroit déjà renouvelé.

## THE NORMAL IMPULSE

Behind each head, notes of the clarion, flashing of electric lights.
Legs, arms, face muscles twitching until the person cannot be recognized.
Then the low-lying silence, night and truth.
In front of each head a white mask, a wisecrack, the soul unmoving.
The eye lingers over each feature, over the limpid line and the whole body.
Cold calm.
And at the same moment, no one saying them, vague words set forth.
The lips tremble.
Everything which can deceive will come to be.

## SOUL AND BODY SUPERPOSED

In the bedroom the sick mind and the prone body.
The flame pierces.
The triangle of the lamp on the ceiling lines up with the next room.
Once all the pains are parallel, there's no escape.
When there's no hope for anything but the last drop, the last instant, the chain is lifted.
I examine the triangle with a vision distorted by fever and by heartbeats that guide the danger.
On the wall opposite the mirror — that icy black abyss ruled by a threatening void and an equally threatening silence: the likelihood of every possible laceration — I can glimpse blessed landscapes smiling under sunbeams, luminous bells, shouts filling the air, many different colors, brilliant gusts against an overloaded sky.
But within the oval holding my whole countenance frozen, my memory anxious, lacerated, spent by constantly renewed efforts — just then I have the precise notion of time regained, of someone coming, and the limit of our chaotic movements in that narrow space already renewed.

J'ai perdu ce caractère blanc qui dirigeait les toits. L'esprit des toits, les girouettes — et la pointe des doigts.

En même temps nous avons perdu toutes les lignes qui reliaient les étoiles du ciel et le ciel à la terre. Les lignes de métal. Tous les préparatifs sont faits, les oiseaux partent, quittent la terre pour un autre pavé.

Les gardes des courants réguliers sont là, les cavaliers sont là et moi je perds la tête dans ce vent qui entraîne le chemin ouvert et la poussière à travers des pays que l'on ne connaît pas. On voit dans la glace de l'eau les hommes déformés. Je crois qu'ils avancent. Majs le courant inverse les ramène, les plie ou les laisse flotter. Ce ne sont pourtant que des images. Les images des hommes déformées dans un grand courant d'air ou un autre mirage.

Et pas à pas — ils avancent plus près — contre le bord du cadre au dur visage.

## WALKING BESIDE DEATH

I have lost this white figure which guided the roofs. The spirits of the roofs, the weathervanes — and the tips of the fingers.

At the same time we have lost all the lines linking the stars of the sky and sky to earth. The metal lines. All the preparations are done, the birds are taking flight, leaving the earth for another pavement.

The guards of the regular currents are present, and the horsemen, and I myself lose my head in the wind which sweeps away the open path and the dust across countries as yet unknown. In the water's mirror deformed men are seen. I think they are coming forward. But the opposing current brings them back, bends them, or lets them float. Yet these are only images. The images of men deformed in a great draught of air or another mirage.

And step by step — they are coming closer — against the edge of the frame with the hard face.

Dans l'abîme doré, rouge, glacé, doré, l'abîme où gîte la douleur, les tourbillons roulants entraînent les bouillons de mon sang dans les vases, dans les retours de flammes de mon tronc. La tristesse moirée s'engloutit dans les crevasses tendres du cœur. Il y a des accidents obscurs et compliqués, impossibles à dire. Et il y a pourtant l'esprit de l'ordre, l'esprit régulier, l'esprit commun à tous les désespoirs qui interroge. O toi qui traînes sur la vie, entre les buissons fleuris et pleins d'épines de la vie, parmi les feuilles mortes, lesr reliefs de triomphes, les appels sans secours, les balayures morderées, la poudre sèche des espoirs, les braises noircies de la gloire, et les coups de révolte, toi, qui ne voudrais plus désormais aboutir nulle part. Toi, source intarissable de sang. Toi, désastre intense de lueurs qu'aucun jet de source, qu'aucun glacier rafraîchissant ne tentera jamais d'éteindre de sa sève. Toi, lumière. Toi, sinuosité de l'amour enseveli qui se dérobe. Toi, parure des ciels cloués sur les poutres de l'infini. Plafond des idées contradictoires. Vertigineuse pesée des forces ennemies. Chemins mêlés dans le fracas des chevelures. Toi, douceur et haine — horizon ébréché, ligne pure de l'indifférence et de l'oubli. Toi, ce matin, tout seul dans l'ordre, le calme et la révolution universelle. Toi, clou de diamant. Toi, pureté, pivot éblouissant du flux et du reflux de ma pensée dans les lignes du monde.

## THE HEAD FILLED WITH BEAUTY

In the gilded abyss, crimson, frozen, gilded, the abyss where sorrow shelters, the twisting whirlwinds entice my boiling blood into the slime, into the tortuous flames of my trunk. Sadness in moire pattern is swallowed up in the heart's tender crevasses. Obscure and complicated accidents take place, impossible to describe. And nevertheless the spirit of order, the even spirit, the spirit common to all despairs is questioning. Oh, as you walk through life, between the flowering and thorn-filled shrubs of life, among the dead leaves, the outlines of triumph, the helpless appeals, the bronze dust sweepings, the dry powder of hopes, the blackened embers of fame, and the revolt, you would never desire an end anywhere, ever again. You, unquenchable source of blood. You, disaster intense with gleams which no surging spring, no cooling glacier will ever try to extinguish with its sap. You, light. You, sinuosity of buried love, hiding. You, ornament of heavens nailed upon the pilings of the infinite. Ceiling of contradictory ideas. Vertiginous balance of enemy forces. Paths confused in the fray of hair. You, gentleness and hatred — horizon chipped away, pure line of indifference and oblivion. You, this morning, totally alone in order, calm, and universal revolution. You, diamond nail. You, purity, dazzling swivel of the ebb and flow of my thought in the lines of the world.

Selection from

# *Sources du Vent*
# *(Wind Sources)*

1929

Collected in *Main d'oeuvre*

Translated by

Mary Ann Caws and Patricia Terry

## LUMIÈRE ROUSSE

On accroche le ciel d'automne aux quatre coins
          Un tambour résonne
Des pas dans le vent
              Le regard qu'on donne
              A chaque passant
Les flammes effilées à travers les barrières
                  Les maisons retournées
                  Tous les dos en prières
Et les jours perdus dans les aventures
                  le long des années
Il n'y a pas de temps
Mais de la poussière
ou l'eau du printemps
dans chaque clairière au regard ardent
Sous les flocons plus lourds
Sous le poids des nuages
Il reste encore un tour à faire sur la page
Un nom qui se traîne
Un cœur qui s'en va
Ce n'est pas la peine
De s'arrêter là
              Personne dans la marge
Plus rien sur le trottoir
              Le ciel est plein d'orages
              Ma tête sans espoir

## RUSSET LIGHT

They are hanging the autumn sky by its four corners
                    A drum is beating
Footsteps in the wind
                    The look they give
                    Every passer-by
The tapered flames through the barriers
                    The houses with their backs
                    Toward us, in prayer
And the days wasted in adventures
                    along the years
There is no time
But there is dust
or springtime water
in each clearing with its ardent look
Under the heavier snowflakes
Under the weight of the clouds
There is still another move to make on the page
A name hanging on
A heart leaving
There's no use
Stopping there
                    No one in the margin
Nothing left on the sidewalk
                    The sky is full of storms
                    My head without hope

GALERIES

Un entonnoir immense où se tordait la nuit
      Des lambeaux s'échappaient par moments
Des lueurs qui allaient s'éteindre bien plus loin
          Tout était pâle
  L'aube
  Le soleil naissant
  Une boule à peine ronde
  Le reflet du monde
  Sur l'écran
Une ligne horizontale se tendait
      L'air se mettait à vibrer
     Il fallait attendre
Les voix qui revenaient de loin
    Rappelaient ta vie en arrière
Mais le chemin qu'il aurait fallu refaire était trop long
Les voix familières trop tristes
Les yeux qui te regardent sont sinistres
     On ne peut plus avancer
Toutes les portes sont fermées
Derrière quelqu'un écoute plaqué contre le mur
    Et le rideau qui tremble
  retombe
Il te ressemble
      Le centre se déplace
Les parois inclinées rendent le ciel plus grand
    L'ombre déborde
     La tête se penchait
C'est celle d'un malade
Et la seule qui existait
Une étoile se déclouait
    Tout près
La main lentement se soulève
Le front plissé a dissipé son rêve
Et tout ce qui derrière était passé
    Une seule fois
     dans le temps qui s'amasse

# GALLERIES

In an immense funnel night was twisting
  From time to time a shred broke loose
Glimmers which would die out much further on
      Everything was pale
  The dawn
  The rising sun
  A sphere scarcely round
  The reflection of the world
  On the screen
A horizontal line extended
    The air began to vibrate
    You had to wait
The voices returning from afar
    Called back your life
The path you travelled would have been too long to take again
The familiar voices too sad
The eyes looking at you are sinister
   We can't go further
All the doors are closed
Behind someone is listening pressed against the wall
   And the curtain trembling
        falls back down
He looks like you
    The center is displaced
The slanting walls make the sky bigger
    The shadow spills over
     The head leaning down
The head of a sick man
     The only one there is
    A star dropped off
  Very near
Slowly the hand rises
The furrowed brow has sent its dream away
And behind it all that had taken place
   Just once
   In the accumulation of time

On ne regarde pas
          C'est à recommencer
Mais quand pourra-t-on revenir
Au moment où tout peut finir
          La vie entière est en jeu
Constamment
Nous passons à côté du vide élégamment
                    sans tomber
Mais parfois quelque chose en nous fait tout trembler
Et le monde n'existe plus
          Nos yeux se trompent
L'on n'entend plus le même son
La même voix
C'est derrière l'univers soi-même que l'on voit
          Une silhouette qui danse
La série de portraits qui ne rappellent rien
          De ceux que l'on ne connaît pas
Ce sont des gens qui vous regardent
          Des cadres éclatants les gardent
Au milieu de ces visages immobiles
Le seul qui soit vivant
               Paraît le plus tranquille
Il part pour ne plus revenir
Dans la salle où les murs se sont mis à sourire
Il n'y a plus que la nuit qui monte pour sortir
     Un pas résonnant sur la dalle
Il fait froid
Ton regard levé vers les étoiles

Nobody's watching
   We have to begin again
But when can we return
Just when everything can end
    All of life is at stake
Always
We walk by the abyss elegantly
     and we don't fall
But at times something inside us makes everything tremble
And the world no longer exists
       Our eyes are mistaken
We don't hear the same sound
The same voice
It's behind the universe ourselves we see
  A silhouette dancing
The series of portraits recalling nothing
  Of those whom we don't know
They are people looking at you
      Striking frames contain them
Among these unmoving faces
The only living one
     Seems the most tranquil
He leaves never to return
In the room where the walls have begun to smile
Only night is left rising to leave
  A step sounding on the stones
It's cold
Your gaze lifted toward the stars

## MOUVANT PAYSAGE

Levé
Le chant plus haut

      On part
Le ciel a déridé son front
        Peut-on savoir l'heure qu'il est
Aucune limite n'est fixée
On pourrait traverser la terre
sans jamais s'arrêter

       La nuit
     Les champs s'allongent
     Une lumière vient
Un trou
     Le ciel qui se déchire
     Tout craque
Et l'on n'entend plus rien
     Un passant
     Une étoile tombe
Et les autres qui la regardent
La lune tord son cou par-dessus les arbres

MOVING LANDSCAPE

Risen
The song higher

      We are leaving
The sky has unwrinkled its forehead
      What time is it please
No limit has been fixed
We could cross the earth
without ever stopping

        Night
      The fields are lengthening
      A light is coming
A hole
      The sky tearing open
      Everything cracking
We hear nothing now
      A passerby
      A star is falling
And the others looking at it
The moon cranes its neck above the trees

*Mary Ann Caws*

# HISTOIRE

Une lettre écrite à l'envers
La main qui passe sur ta tête
Et l'heure
Où l'on se lève le matin
Soleil rouillé
Vitre fondue
Nature morte
Le courant d'air ferme ma porte
Et les songes m'ont réveillé

Il y a encore une bougie qui brûle

STORY

A letter written backwards
The hand passing over your head
And the hour
When you get up in the morning
Rusted sun
Melted windowpane
Still life
The draft is closing my door
And the dreams have waked me

There is still one candle burning

*Mary Ann Caws*

## LA LIGNE DES NOMS ET DES FIGURES

Ce soir beau caractère au théâtre des toits
  Pas de signe
        Titre et date
La tête échevelée se cache aux fils de fer qui pendent
     Les étoiles du jour se rendent
Les nuages secouent leurs plumes sur le toit
Et celui qui passe dans le vent aigre n'est pas moi
        Figure sur le mur trop rouge
        Et elle s'allonge
Le soleil perd son sang sur la neige qui fond
      Un homme le ramasse et se masque
        Faux nom
   Le souffle qui gonfle
   Le moteur qui ronfle
Le poète s'essouffle pour arriver le premier
       Il est raide et lourd
Le bord de la terre qui craque
Les murs qui se défont
La poitrine qui saigne
      Derrière
    Un faux plastron
    Grimace
  Ombre que tu effaces
     Les cils vibrent
     Les vitres glissent
     Les volets battent
Le papillon métallique puise la pluie
       et crache l'eau
    à plein moteur
   Le programme est chargé
On reconnaît les noms écrits contre le mur en caractères étrangers
Je pense
  à ton dos ridicule quand tu dors
       et à ton illusion
         de face

# THE LINE OF NAMES AND FIGURES

Tonight the favorable aspect of the Rooftop Theater
   No omen
         Title and date
The disheveled head concealed by dangling iron wires
      Daytime's stars appear
The clouds shake their feathers onto the roof
And it is not I who contends with the harsh wind
        A figure on the all-too-red wall
        That lies down at full length
The sun wastes its blood on the melting snow
      A man gathers it and hides himself
         Not his real name
  Breathing heavily
  The engine rumbles
The poet breathless to be first in line
          He is stiff and heavy
The muddy rim cracks
The walls come apart
His chest is bleeding
      Behind
    A false shirt-front
    Grimaces
A shadow you conceal
      The eyelashes quiver
      The panes slide
      The shutters beat
The metal butterfly sucks up rain
        and spits water
  hard as he can
   The program is full
 We can guess the names written on the wall in foreign
  letters
 I can't help thinking
  of your silly back when you're asleep
       and of your face that's so
             unreal

Selection from

# *Pierres Blanches*
# *(White Stones)*

1930

Collected in *Main d'oeuvre*

Translated by Mary Ann Caws

## MAIS RIEN

Un même pan ferme le coin
Où l'air libre s'étend
Autour la corde glisse
Et l'eau monte
La pluie descend
Un homme tombe de fatigue
C'est le même qui tend sa main
On saute le mur du jardin
Le ciel est plus bas
Le jour baisse
La route court
Et le vent cesse
On pourrait croire qu'il est arrivé quelque chose
Mais rien

## BUT NOTHING

A same side closes the corner
Where the free air stretches out
The rope slips around
And the water rises
The rain comes down
A man falls from fatigue
The same one extending his hand
You leap over the garden wall
The sky is lower
The day is downing
The road is running
And the wind stops
You might think something had happened
But nothing

Selection from

# *Ferraille*
# *(Scrap Iron)*
1937

Collected in *Main d'oeuvre*


Translated by Mary Ann Caws

# REFLUX

Quand le sourire éclatant des façades déchire le décor fragile du matin; quand l'horizon est encore plein du sommeil qui s'attarde, les rêves murmurant dans les ruisseaux des haies; quand la nuit rassemble ses haillons pendus aux basses branches, je sors, je me prepare, je suis plus pâle et plus tremblant que cette page où aucun mot du sort n'était encore inscrit. Toute la distance de vous à moi — de la vie qui tressaille à la surface de ma main au sourire mortel de l'amour sur sa fin — chancelle, déchirée. La distance parcourue d'une seule traite sans arrêt, dans les jours sans clarté et les nuits sans sommeil. Et, ce soir, je voudrais, d'un effort surhumain, secouer toute ette épaisseur de rouille — cette roulle affamée qui déforme mon coeur et me ronge les mains. Pourquoi rester si longtemps enseveli sous les décombres des jours et de la nuit, la poussière des ombres. Et pourquoi tant d'amour et pourquoi tant de haine. Un sang léger bouillonne à grandes vagues dans des vases de prix. Il court dans les fleuves du corps, donnant à la santé toutes les illusions de la victoire. Mais le voyageur exténué, ébloui, hypnotisé par les lueurs fascinantes des phares, donrt debout, il ne résise plus aux passes magnétiques de la mort. Ce soir je voudrais dépenser tout l'or de la mémoire, deposer mes bagages trop lourds. Il n'y a plus devant mes yeux que le ciel nu, les murs de la prison qui enserrait ma tête, les pavés de la rue. Il faut remonter du plus bas de la mine, de la terre épaissie par l'humus du malheur, reprendre l'air dans les recoins les plus obscurs de la poitrine, pousser vers les hauteurs — où la glace étincelle de tous les feux croisés de l'incendie — où la neige ruisselle, le caractère dur, dans les tempêtes sans tendresse de l'égoïsme et les décisions tranchantes de l'esprit.

# EBB

When the dazzling smile of façades tears apart morning's fragile setting; when the horizon is still full of lingering sleep, dreams murmuring in the streams of hedges; when night picks up its tatters draped on the lowest branches, I go out, I ready myself, I am paler and more trembling than this page, where no fateful word had yet been inscribed. The entire distance from you to me — from life quivering on the surface of my hand to the mortal smile of love coming to an end — hesitates, rent asunder. The distance covered in one single stretch, in days without brightness and sleepless nights. And this evening, I should like, with a superhuman effort, to shake off this rusty thickness — this rapacious rust deforms my heart and eats away at my hands. Why stay so long buried under the debris of days and night, the dust of shadows? And why so much love and why so much hatred? A thin blood frothing in great pulses within precious vases. It runs in the body's rivers, conferring on health all the illusions of victory. But the exhausted traveler, stunned, hypnotized by the fascinating lighthouse beams, sleeps standing, no longer resisting the magnetic assaults of death. Tonight I should like to spend all the gold of my memory, put down my bags, now too heavy. Before my eyes nothing but the bare sky, the prison walls which once enclosed my head, the cobblestones of the street. I must rise up again from the lowest depths of the mine, from the earth thicknened by the rich soil of unhappiness, take air back again into the darkest nooks of my chest, thrusting towards the heights — where the ice glitters with all the crossfire of flames — where the snow streams in harsh character, through the untender tempests of egoism and the cutting decisions of the mind.

Selection from

# *Le Chant des Morts (Song of the Dead)*

1944–1948

Translated by Mary Ann Caws

## CHEMIN PERDU – PISTE D'ENVOL

Je me suis étendu sous les piliers de cendre
Et tu t'es élevé sur des colonnes d'or
Aux gouffres du malheur je ne peux plus descendre
Le ciel est dépassé
Il surplombe la mort
Je me suis évadé des lignes trop obscures
Et je ne peux plus revenir
J'ai recouvert de sel les traits de ma figure
Et je n'ai plus de place au monde que j'ai fui
Cherche dans le soleil
Cherche dans les ténèbres
Je cherche dans ton coeur un impossible écho
Vers les trainées d'ennui de l'exil en toi-même
Plus haut


## LONGUE PORTÉE

Poissons dorés surpris dans les mailles du vent
Catapultes de la lumière
Regains de soif lancés dans tous les coins
Détentes révolues des appétits déteints
Tout se mêle dans le remous des ondes prisonnières
La poitrine résonne come un sol creux
Il y a des ombres sur le buvard de tes joues
Et des claquements de porcelaine bleue
Par-dessus tous les toits aux lames de violettes
Un rouge de valeur plus dense sans écho
Un sang plus étendu au flanc de la olline
Des oiseaux migrateurs sans orientation
Et tous ces hommes morts sans rime ni raison
Tant de coeurs desséchés
Sans plomb
Comme des feuilles

## LOST PATH – TAKE-OFF RUNWAY

I stretched out under the pillars of ash
And you rose up on columns of gold
Into the abyss of sorrow I can descend no longer
The sky is exceeded
It overlooks death

I escaped lines too obscure
And I can't return
I've covered with salt the features of my face
And I've no longer a place in the world I fled
Seek in the sun
Seek in the gloom
And seek an impossible echo in your heart
Towards the trails of the boredom of exile in yourself
Higher


## LONG REACH

Gilded fish surprised in the mesh of the wind
Catapults of light
Bygone thirst cast in all the corners
Leisures devolved of faded appetites
All mingles in the swirl of captive waves
The breast resonates like a hollow ground
There are shadows on the blotter of your cheeks
And slammings of blue china
Above all the roofs with violet blades
A red of denser weight without echo
Blood extended further on the hillside
Migrating birds without direction
And all these men dead without rhyme or reason
So many hearts dried
Unleaded
Like leaves

Selection from

# *Bois Vert*
# *(Green Wood)*

1946–1949

Translated by

Mary Ann Caws and Patricia Terry

## DANS CE DÉSERT

Ce dard
Que ton regard m'a laissé dans le flanc
Ce dard qui n'en sort pas
Cette tête inspirée qui tient tout l'horizon
Le plat bord de la nuit
qui me sert de bâillon
Et la soif de bonheur qui me soutenait ma fièvre

Dans ce désert

Enfin rien ne sort
Rien ne vient
Dans la réalité trop somber
Où le soleil déplie son papier de couleur
        toujours neuf
On ignore le jeu et la partie se gagne
Sur le trapèze d'os où le singe s'endort
Encore un cran dans la montée sévère
Et décidément rien ne sort
De ton coeur démonté où la rumeur s'apaise

Rien ne tient à la loi des mots
A la liste des morts au somrneil sans encombre
Arbres couverts de sel
de fruits cueillis dans les ruelles
Têtes charnues plissées de rires pleins d'abeilles
Rien ne tient au fond
Ni à la forme
L'esprit monte à la corde sans effort
Comrne le soleil dans les ombres
Puis je tâche de vivre à mon moindre ressort
Je tâte la nuit qui approche
Comme la mer repue
qui regagne ses bords
Ma nuit sans horizon où la lune s'accroche
Rien ne répond à mon appel muet

## IN THIS DESERT

That glance
which left its sting in my side
And it stays there
That inspired head with the whole horizon inside
The flat edge of night
which I use as a gag
And the thirst for happiness making me feverish

In this desert

At last nothing leaves
Nothing comes in
Reality is too dark
Where the sun unfolds its ever-changing
colored paper
We ignore the game and somebody wins
Where the monkey falls asleep on the bone trapeze
One step higher in the steep climb
And it's true that nothing leaves
From your dismantled heart growing quiet
Nothing cares about words or their laws
The list of the dead sleeping at their ease
Trees covered in salt
From fruits gathered in gutters
Fleshy heads pleated with bee-filled laughter
Nothing cares about meaning
Or style
Without even trying the mind climbs its rope
Like the sun in the shadows
Then I try to live at my lowest level
I grope for the night approaching
As the sea having reached its limit
  withdraws
My horizonless night where the moon finds a place
Nothing answers my mute appeal

Rien ne s' oppose à ce geste durci
qui fauche ma moisson
Allons il fait plus chaud
plus noir dans la maison
Mon coeur a dévidé sa laine
Plus de feu dans le coin
Plus d'amour plus de haine
Bateau perdu sans mât
Sans orientation
Tête tranchée
Poitrine sans passion
Houle du monde nu
Fermé
Cercle de ma prison
Amour sec
Et la mort à secret
Sur la fenêtre bleue
Qui m'attend au balcon
Veilleuse au cadre noir
A l'angle des saisons
Ma part de faim
de soif
mains vides
sang perdu

Dans  ce désert

Nothing opposes this calloused gesture
    which reaps my harvest
Well it's warmer in the house
and darker
My heart has unwound its wool
No more fire in the corner
No more love nor hatred
Shipwrecked without a mast
Without direction
Head cut off
Chest without passion
Groundswell of the bare world
Closed
Circle of my prison
Dry love
And death in secret
On the blue window
Awaits me on the balcony
Nightlight framed in black
At the corner of seasons
My share of hunger
of thirst
empty hands
blood spilled

In this desert

Selection from

*Au Soleil du plafond
(The Sun on the Ceiling)*
1955


Translated by

Mary Ann Caws and Patricia Terry

## MUSICIEN

L'ombre, le musicien, l'immense rideau bleu qui partage l'espace.
C'est son nom qui frappe le battant, c'est l'air qui glisse mieux. Assis
sur le versant profound d'une colline, entre les murs en creux,
j'entends courir les signes plus vite que mes yeux. Entre les murs,
devant le ciel, la fenêtre au milieu, les pieds sur le tapis où
s'éteignent les étincelles, ou les étoiles, ou quelques autres signes
lumineux.


## LA LAMPE

Le vent noir qui tordait les rideaux ne pouvait soulever le papier ni eteindre
la lampe.

Dans un courant de peur, il semblait que quelqu'un put entrer. Entre la porte
ouverte et le volet qui bat — personne ! Et pourtant sur la table ébranlée une
clarté remue dans cette chambre vide.


## MASQUE

Au fond du verre, l'oeil fixe, le ruban, la goutte d'or et un regard qui tremble.
Tout le monde est parti. Ce triste carnival entre l'hiver et l'âtre, le soleil réchauf-
fant. La pluie tombe plus doucement, la mer se décolore et le visage dur redevient
transparent. Sous les traits découverts, la tête est à la mode. Et même dans la glace
contre le paravent. Ma mémoire en désordre.

## THE MUSICIAN

The shadow, the musician, the immense blue curtain dividing space.
It's his name which beats, it's the air which glides more smoothly. Seated on
the steepest slope of a hill, between the hollow walls, I hear the sounds of the
signs running by quicker than my eyes. Between the walls, facing the sky,
with the window in the middle, his feet on the carpet, where the sparks are
fading, or the stars, or some other luminous signs.


## THE LAMP

The black wind twisting the curtains couldn't lift the paper or put out the
lamp.
Fear was sweeping through — it seemed that someone could have come in.
Between the open door and the shutter clacking — no one! And on the still shak-
ing table a radiance stirs in the empty room.


## MASK

At the bottom of the glass, the staring eye, the ribbon, the golden drop and
a trembling glance. Everyone has left. This sad carnival between winter and the
hearth, the sun warming. The rain falls more gently, the sea grows pale, and the
harsh visage becomes transparent once more. Under the features now uncov-
ered, the head is in fashion. And even in the mirror against the screen. My mem-
ory is in disarray.

## PENDULE

Dans l'air chaud du plafond la rampe des rêves s'allume.

Les murs blancs se sont arrondis. La poitrine oppressée souffle des mots con-
fus. Dans la glace, tourne le vent du sud chargé de feuilles et de plumes. La fenêtre
est bouchée. Le cœur est à peu près éteint parmi les cendres déjà froides de la
lune — les mains sont sans abri — tous les arbres couchés. Dans le vent du désert
les aiguilles s'inclinent et mon heure est passée.

## PENDULUM

In the warm air of the ceiling, the stage of dreams lights up.

The white walls are round now. The suffocating chest breathes out confused words. In the mirror the south wind turns, weighed down with leaves and feathers. The window is blocked. The heart is almost extinguished among the ashes of the moon already cold — the hands have nowhere to hide — all the trees are laid flat. In the desert wind the clock's hands give in and my time has passed.

Selection from

# *La Liberté des Mers*
# *(The Freedom of the Seas)*
1960

Translated by

Mary Ann Caws and Patricia Terry

## LA TRAME

Une main, d'un mouvement rythmique
et sans pensée, jetait ses cinq doigts vers
le plafond où dansaient des ombres fantastiques.
Une main détachée du bras, une main
libre, éclairée par la lueur du foyer qui
venait de plus bas — et cette tête innocente
et vide qui souriait à l'araignée activant
dans la nuit son chef-d'œuvre inutile.

## SANS ENTRER

Derrière la porte sans vitres, deux têtes
de remords s'encadrent dans un sinistre jeu
de grimace amicale. Et par l'autre porte
entr'ouverte — celle qui les protège assez
mal de la nuit — on aperçoit le rayon où
s'alignent les livres, où se réfugient les rires
et les mots des veillées sous la lampe, sous
la garde d'un très vieux portrait — menaçant
de son éternel sourire équivoque.
Et tout s'étouffe et s'assoupit en attendant
le réveil, la lumière et la vie, et, plus que
tout, la fin de l'effroyable rêve.

## THE WEB

A hand, with a rhythmic and thoughtless motion,
was throwing its five fingers up towards the ceiling
where fantastic shadows were dancing.
A hand detached from its arm, a free hand,
illumined from below by the glow of the hearth —
and that innocent empty head smiling at the spider
setting forth in the night its useless masterpiece.


## WITHOUT GOING IN

Behind the opaque door, two heads
of remorse are framed in a sinister play
of amicable expression. And through the other door
half-opened — offering them scarce protection
from the night — one sees a shelf
with its row of books, where laughter
and words of long evenings by lamplight take shelter,
watched over by a very old portrait — threatening
in its fixed equivocal smile.
And everything is stifled and drowsy, waiting for
the waking, for light and life, and, more than anything,
for the horrendous dream to end.

## SOUFFLE

Il neige sur mon toit et sur les arbres. Le
mur et le jardin sont blancs, le sentier noir
et la maison s'est écroulée sans bruit. Il neige.

## BREATH

It is snowing on my roof and on the trees.
The wall and the garden are white, the path black,
and the house has given way without a sound.
It is snowing.

*Our special thanks to Etienne-Alain Hubert*
*and to Jaime Shearn Coan*
*for their most valued assistance in this publication.*

# PIERRE REVERDY – BIBLIOGRAPHY

## Volumes from which the translations are taken

*Selected Poems: Pierre Reverdy*, tr. Kenneth Rexroth. London: Jonathan Cape, 1969; New York: New Directions, 1972.

*Roof Slates and Other Poems of Pierre Reverdy*, tr. Mary Ann Caws and Patricia Terry. Boston: Northeastern University Press, 1981.

*Pierre Reverdy: Selected Poems* by Mary Ann Caws, ed. Timothy Bent, tr. John Ashbery, Mary Ann Caws & Patricia Terry. Winston-Salem, N.C.: Wake Forest University Press, 1991.

*Prose Poems*, tr. Ron Padgett. Brooklyn, N.Y.: Black Square Editions and the Brooklyn Rail, 2007.


## Volumes on which the information relies

*Pierre Reverdy: Oeuvres complètes, tomes I , II, III*, ed. Etienne-Alain Hubert, Flammarion, 2010.

*Bibliographie des Écrits de Pierre Reverdy*, ed. Etienne-Alain Hubert. Comité Pierre Reverdy de la Fondation Maeght/Éditions des Cendres. 2011.

*La Main de Pierre Reverdy* by Mary Ann Caws, Droz, 1979.

# TESTIMONIES

From *Pierre Reverdy, 1889–1960* (Mercure de France, 1962)

Louis Aragon, writing about *Les Ardoises du toit*: "Rather than naming what he sees, he prefers to say what is missing: each absence afflicts him and troubles him intimately…he is haunted by the conditional… As he is the poet of fear and silence, Pierre Reverdy is the poet of night…" (SIC, no. 29, May 1918.)

Louis Aragon: "A Black Sun has set in Solesmes"

"No one notices this unknown person so apart, the sun turns and his shadow grows, extends, covers the century…I've spent what I could steal from this terrible day reading a great book of 12 years ago, a great book which Picasso decorated with thick red lines, as if he had for his friend Reverdy dipped his thumb in his blood. It is called *Le Chant des morts (The Song of the Dead)*, and who has ever spoken like this of death."

John Ashbery on "Reverdy in America"

"Here and there in America, there are poets for whom the name of Reverdy is full of magic… for Frank O'Hara, in 'A Step Away from Them,' his name is a sort of talisman… and for Kenneth Koch… Reverdy is a spiritual guide.

"On the several poets who have heard Reverdy's lesson, the effect has been profound and it may have repercussions in American poetry… Reverdy manages to give back to things their real name, so annul the eternal dead weight of symbolism and allegory…

It is strange that America, with its reputation of energy and rapid annexation, has produced such a phlegmatic and conventional poetry, while France, considered as the country of the intellectuals, has given us Reverdy… His immediate character is so near to the spontaneity which has always marked the best of America's production — from Whitman to Pollock — in literature and art."

# ABOUT THE TRANSLATORS

Editor and translator MARY ANN CAWS is an American author, art historian, translator, and literary critic. Distinguished Professor of English, French, and Comparative Literature at the Graduate School at the City University of New York, Caws is one of the leading authorities on and translators of Dada, Surrealism, and art movements of that time period. Her many books and writings are published around the world and she lectures widely.

PATRICIA TERRY was professor of French Literature at Barnard College and later at the University of California at San Diego. A celebrated translator, among whose renderings are *The Song of Roland* and *Poems of the Elder Edda* (The Middle Ages Series). Her last published titles include *Capital of Pain* by Paul Eluard (with Mary Ann Caws and Nancy Kline), *Essential Poems and Prose of Jules Laforgue*, *The Sea and Other Poems* by Guillevic (with Monique Chefdor), and *Selected Prose and Poetry of Jules Supervielle* (with Nancy Kline and Kathleen Micklow).

*A Life of Poems, Poems of a Life* by Anna de Noailles. Translated by Norman R. Shapiro. Introduction by Catherine Perry.

*Approximate Man and Other Writings* by Tristan Tzara. Translated and edited by Mary Ann Caws.

*Art Poétique* by Guillevic. Translated by Maureen Smith.

*The Big Game* by Benjamin Péret. Translated with an introduction by Marilyn Kallet.

*Capital of Pain* by Paul Eluard. Translated by Mary Ann Caws, Patricia Terry, and Nancy Kline.

*Chanson Dada: Selected Poems* by Tristan Tzara. Translated with an introduction and essay by Lee Harwood.

*Essential Poems and Writings of Joyce Mansour: A Bilingual Anthology.* Translated with an introduction by Serge Gavronsky.

*Essential Poems and Prose of Jules Laforgue.* Translated and edited by Patricia Terry.

*Essential Poems and Writings of Robert Desnos: A Bilingual Anthology.* Edited with an introduction and essay by Mary Ann Caws.

*EyeSeas (Les Ziaux)* by Raymond Queneau. Translated with an introduction by Daniela Hurezanu and Stephen Kessler.

*Fables in a Modern Key* by Pierre Coran. Edited and translated by Norman R. Shapiro. Color illustrations by Olga Pastuchiv.

*Furor and Mystery & Other Writings* by René Char. Edited and translated by Mary Ann Caws and Nancy Kline.

*Guarding the Air: Selected Poems of Gunnar Harding.* Translated and edited by Roger Greenwald.

*The Inventor of Love & Other Writings* by Gherasim Luca. Translated by Julian & Laura Semilian. Introduction by Andrei Codrescu. Essay by Petre Răileanu.

*Jules Supervielle: Selected Prose and Poetry.* Translated by Nancy Kline and Patricia Terry.

*La Fontaine's Bawdy* by Jean de La Fontaine. Translated with an introduction by Norman R. Shapiro.

*Last Love Poems of Paul Eluard.* Translated with an introduction by Marilyn Kallet.

*Love, Poetry (L'amour la poésie)* by Paul Eluard. Translated with an essay by Stuart Kendall.

*Pierre Reverdy: Poems Early to Late.* Translated by Mary Ann Caws and Patricia Terry.

*Poems of André Breton: A Bilingual Anthology.* Translated with essays by Jean-Pierre Cauvin and Mary Ann Caws.

*Poems of A.O. Barnabooth* by Valéry Larbaud. Translated by Ron Padgett and Bill Zavatsky.

*Poems of Consummation* by Vicente Aleixandre. Translated by Stephen Kessler.

*Préversities: A Jacques Prévert Sampler.* Translated and edited by Norman R. Shapiro.

*The Sea and Other Poems* by Guillevic. Translated by Patricia Terry. Introduction by Monique Chefdor.

*To Speak, to Tell You? Poems* by Sabine Sicaud. Translated by Norman R. Shapiro. Introduction and notes by Odile Ayral-Clause.

## Forthcoming Translations

*Boris Vian Invents Boris Vian: A Boris Vian Reader.* Edited and translated by Julia Older.

*Earthlight (Claire de Terre)* by André Breton. Translated by Bill Zavatsky and Zack Rogrow. (New and revised edition.)

*Reality and Desire (La realidad y el deseo): New Selected Poems of Luis Cernuda.* Translated by Stephen Kessler.

*The Gentle Genius of Cécile Périn: Selected Poems (1906–1956).* Edited and translated by Norman R. Shapiro.

# MODERN POETRY SERIES

*ABC of Translation* by Willis Barnstone

*An Alchemist with One Eye on Fire*
by Clayton Eshleman

*Anticline* by Clayton Eshleman

*Archaic Design* by Clayton Eshleman

*Backscatter: New and Selected Poems* by John Olson

*Barzakh (Poems 2000–2012)* by Pierre Joris

*The Caveat Onus* by Dave Brinks

*City Without People: The Katrina Poems*
by Niyi Osundare

*Concealments and Caprichos* by Jerome Rothenberg

*Crusader-Woman* by Ruxandra Cesereanu.
Translated by Adam J. Sorkin. Introduction
by Andrei Codrescu.

*Curdled Skulls: Poems of Bernard Bador.*
Translated by the author with Clayton Eshleman.

*Endure: Poems* by Bei Dao. Translated by
Clayton Eshleman and Lucas Klein.

*Exile is My Trade: A Habib Tengour Reader.*
Translated by Pierre Joris.

*Eye of Witness: A Jerome Rothenberg Reader.*
Edited with commentaries by Heriberto Yepez
& Jerome Rothenberg.

*Fire Exit* by Robert Kelly

*Forgiven Submarine* by Ruxandra Cesereanu and
Andrei Codrescu

*from stone this running* by Heller Levinson

*The Grindstone of Rapport:*
*A Clayton Eshleman Reader*

*Larynx Galaxy* by John Olson

*The Love That Moves Me* by Marilyn Kallet

*Memory Wing* by Bill Lavender

*Packing Light: New and Selected Poems*
by Marilyn Kallet

*The Present Tense of the World: Poems 2000–2009*
by Amina Saïd. Translated with an introduction by
Marilyn Hacker.

*The Price of Experience* by Clayton Eshleman

*The Secret Brain: Selected Poems 1995–2012*
by Dave Brinks

*Signal from Draco: New and Selected Poems*
by Mebane Robertson

## Forthcoming Modern Poetry Titles

*An American Unconscious* by Mebane Robertson

*Disenchanted City (La Ville desenchantee)* by
Chantal Bizzini. Edited by Marilyn Kallet and
J. Bradford Anderson. Translated by J. Bradford
Anderson, Darren Jackson, and Marilyn Kallet.

*Essential Poetry (1968–2015)* by Clayton Eshleman

*Funny Way of Staying Alive* by Willis Barnstone

*The Hexagon* by Robert Kelly

*Memory* by Bernadette Mayer

*Soraya (Sonnets)* by Anis Shivani

*Wrack Lariat* by Heller Levinson

## LITERARY THEORY / BIOGRAPHY SERIES

*Clayton Eshleman: The Whole Art* by Stuart Kendall

*Revolution of the Mind: The Life of André Breton*
by Mark Polizzotti

## Forthcoming

*Barbaric Vast & Wild: A Gathering of Outside and
Subterranean Poetry* (*Poems for the Millennium*, vol 5)
Edited by Jerome Rothenberg and
John Bloomberg-Rissman.

WWW.BLACKWIDOWPRESS.COM